LENA CORWIN'S

MADE BY HAND

photography by
Maria Alexandra Vettese and
Stephanie Congdon Barnes

STC CRAFT | A Melanie Falick Book

Stewart, Tabori & Chang | NEW YORK

Published in 2013 by Stewart, Tabori & Chang
An imprint of ABRAMS.

Text copyright © 2013 by Lena Corwin
Illustrations copyright © 2013 by Lena Corwin
Photographs copyright © 2013 by More & Co.

Cataloging-in-Publication Data has been applied
for and is available from the Library of Congress:
ISBN: 978-1-61769-059-4

Editor: Liana Allday
Designer: Brooke Reynolds for inchmark
Production Manager: Tina Cameron

The text of this book was composed in Fournier.

Printed and bound in China.
10 9 8 7 6 5 4 3 2 1

Stewart, Tabori & Chang books are available at special discounts when purchased
in quantity for premiums and promotions as well as fundraising or educational
use. Special editions can also be created to specification. For details, contact
specialsales@abramsbooks.com or the address below.

115 West 18th Street
New York, NY 10011
www.abramsbooks.com

For my talented and inspiring friends.

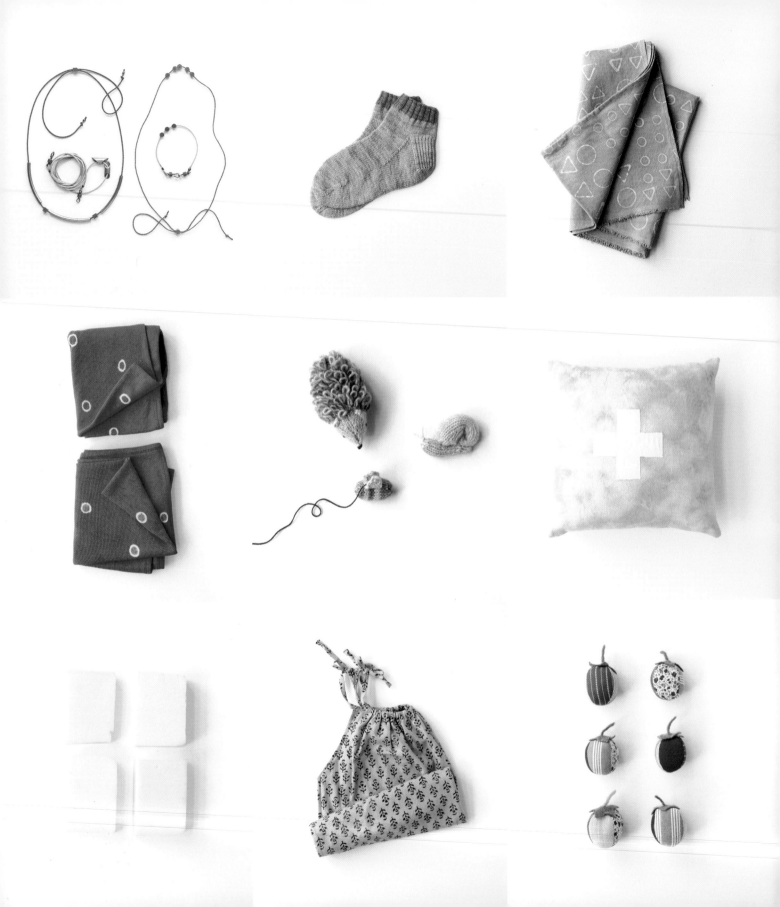

CONTENTS

INTRODUCTION

In 2009, I moved my small, ground-level studio to a much larger space: the light-filled top floor of our Brooklyn brownstone. It felt like a luxury—especially by New York City standards—to have 900 square feet in which to work as a textile designer and illustrator. To make the most of this new space, I decided to start teaching and hosting classes for people who wanted to learn how to make things by hand. The first classes I offered were based on the printing techniques in my book *Printing by Hand*. Soon after I started asking designer friends to teach classes based on the work they do professionally. The classes came together in a natural way, oftentimes based on suggestions from students, and as an added bonus they sparked many new friendships and professional collaborations.

I decided which classes to hold based simply on the skills and projects I wanted to learn myself. From sewing and patternmaking to jewelry and crochet, the classes were diverse—we even had a class on how to make a customized blend of perfume. Each class had different spatial needs, and my open studio space allowed me to reconfigure the room to accommodate the lesson. For instance, the introduction to screen printing class was limited to five students, since each person needed a large amount of space at my long printing table. But we could fit lots of people into Cal Patch's embroidery class since each student only needed a small section of the table. I would push two tables together to make one big surface and we would all sit facing one another, talking as we stitched. (To take Cal's embroidery "class" in this book, turn to page 69.)

(To take Cal's embroidery "class" in this book, turn to page 69.)

Students often told me they signed up for classes because they wanted a break from being on the computer all day. The classes required them to slow down as they developed a new skill, and the methodical nature of handwork was a welcome change. Of course, learning a new craft can be awkward at first, and sometimes students felt impatient. When I took Shabd Simon-Alexander's dyeing class, for instance, I felt frustrated because there seemed to be so many unknowns that could affect the outcome of each piece. After several sessions with Shabd, however, I finally felt that I could control my results. (See pages 133 and 137 to learn some of Shabd's dyeing techniques.) This breakthrough point—when a new skill finally clicks—is something I always love seeing my students experience.

(See pages 133 and 137 to learn some of Shabd's dyeing techniques.)

The sewing classes we offered in the studio were favorites of mine. Jenny Gordy and Wendy Hanson designed patterns specifically for their classes (much like they did for the children's clothing on page 81 and the women's dress and top on page 29), and they expertly helped students learn how to customize the details of their garments. In addition to embroidery classes, Cal also held Saturday sewing workshops in which she taught students how to follow store-bought patterns (something I had always wanted to learn myself). My own sewing skills improved greatly while taking these classes, and I picked up countless tips from Cal, Jenny, and Wendy. I've included a lot of these bits of wisdom in the book, since I'm sure they'll be helpful to you, too.

In early 2011, when my son, Eli, was an infant, I decided to stop teaching and hosting classes. It became too challenging to run the classes while keeping up with my work commitments and the demands of being a new parent. I miss the bustle of people in and out of my studio, as well as the time I spent on such fun and absorbing projects. Since the classes ended, I have received requests from around the world to teach. While traveling and teaching crafts does sound very appealing, that idea has never come to fruition—but it did lead to the idea of teaching classes in the form of a book.

The twenty-six classes presented here are all based on projects that captivate me—some are new fascinations, like brick-stitch beading, while others have intrigued me my whole life, like sewing clothing. They are things I daydream about making while I'm busy with the necessities of daily life. Most of the projects are based on classes that I held in my studio—with the addition of a few that I wanted to offer but never did. And while all of the projects are based on classic craft techniques, they are showcased in new, modern styles, like batik dyeing with geometric shapes instead of more traditional freeform lines, or using fabric instead of paper for origami. All of the teachers in this book have an appreciation for fine craftsmanship and a respect for art forms from the past. Many of us were taught our skills by older family members and family friends. We also all feel strongly that perfection is not the goal—in fact, it is often the imperfections that bring beauty to handmade goods. I hope you will be creative with these projects and make them your own by experimenting with different fabrics or yarns, colors, textures, and patterns.

The projects range in difficulty and some are a bit more complex than others, but I hope you will be inspired to try them all. The instructions are written in plain English, so there's no special lingo or shorthand you'll need to know before you get started, and each teacher was photographed while making her project in order to create the very helpful how-to images in the instructions. Plus an illustrated special techniques section is included on page 168 to give additional instruction for a few of the techniques, such as basic knitting, crocheting, and sewing. As you read and make things from this book, I hope you feel a little bit like you are sitting across the table from the teacher, learning new skills while you create something beautiful by hand.

MEET THE TEACHERS

LENA CORWIN

Rotary-Printed Cloth Napkins, page 17
Screen-Printed Multicolor Fabric, page 23

Lena moved to New York in 1997 and worked in fashion, graphics, and textile design. In 2005, she started her own business, which focused mainly on hand-printed textiles. Her book *Printing by Hand*, an instructional craft book teaching the techniques of printing with stamps, stencils, and silk screens, was published in 2008. That year she also began teaching and hosting classes in her studio.

lenacorwin.com

JENNY GORDY

Sewn Dress and Top, page 29
Knitted Socks, page 35

Jenny worked as a technical designer and fit model in New York City before studying patternmaking at the Fashion Institute of Technology. She started her company, Wiksten—in which she sells her clothing, knitwear, and patterns—in 2005. Jenny works with natural fibers and her clothing is known for its clean lines, impeccable craftsmanship, and wearability. She lives in Iowa City, IA.

wikstenmade.com

CAL PATCH

Crocheted or Braided Rugs, page 63
Embroidery Sampler, page 69

Cal sews, crochets, embroiders, prints, spins, knits, dyes, and more. She designs one-off pieces for her Hodge Podge Farm line, and her book, *Design-It-Yourself Clothes*, was published in 2009. She offers classes in the Hudson Valley through her roving craft school, Double Knot Studio, and travels frequently to teach at retreats and events. Cal lives in Accord, NY.

hodgepodgefarm.net

WENDY HANSON

Fabric Origami, page 75
Sewn Children's Tops and Bottoms, page 81

Wendy is an artist and a formally trained apparel designer and patternmaker. She has worked for Vivienne Westwood, Tibi, Donna Karan, and Daryl K, and she often travels internationally to oversee production development for garments. Her fine arts background greatly informs her design aesthetic as well as her personal projects and art. Wendy lives in Atlanta, GA.

wendy-hanson.com

LIANE TYRREL

Tea-Dyed Appliqué Cross Pillow, page 41
Olive Oil Soap, page 45

In 2008, Liane started her online shop, Enhabiten, where she sells her hand-dyed and sewn home goods and accessories made exclusively from vintage and environmentally sustainable materials. She believes that making things is what she is meant to do, and she loves that the possibilities are endless (and endlessly interesting). Liane lives in Henniker, NH.

etsy.com/shop/enhabiten

CAITLIN MOCIUN

Hand-Painted Children's Leggings, page 51
Batik-Dyed Beach Blanket, page 57

Caitlin studied textile design at Rhode Island School of Design and started her clothing line, Mociun, soon after graduating. In 2012, she opened a shop in Brooklyn selling her own fine jewelry and textiles as well as work from other artists. Her business focuses on environmentally healthy production, and much of her inspiration is drawn from her childhood in California, Prague, and Malaysia. Caitlin lives in Brooklyn, NY.

mociun.com

JENNIFER SARKILAHTI

Brass and Silk Jewelry, page 87
Brick-Stitch Beaded Necklaces, page 93

In 2006, Jennifer started her jewelry company, Odette New York. She designs and crafts her jewelry by hand in her Brooklyn studio employing both ancient and modern wax carving techniques to cast various metals, such as recycled sterling silver, brass, bronze, and gold. Her jewelry is sold in stores around the world and on her website. She lives in Brooklyn, NY.

odetteny.com

JAIME RUGH

Beeswax Birthday Candles, page 99
Woven Placemats, page 103

Jaime attended art schools in Philadelphia and Baltimore, and then spent years in New York City and Los Angeles, working as an artist, artist assistant, florist, shop buyer, and shop decorator. Over the past five years, while caring for her two children, she has worked out of her home as a writer and visual artist, painting, collaging, weaving, and sculpting. She lives in South Orange, NJ.

jaimerugh.bigcartel.com

EMILY EIBEL

Knitted Cat Toys, page 107
Marbled Scarves and Handkerchiefs, page 115

Emily moved to Brooklyn in 2000 to study at Pratt Institute. After graduating, she began illustrating in two distinct directions—a stitched, fiber-focused style and a digital style that is as influenced by folk art as it is by video games. In 2009, Emily began working as an assistant designer for the Martha Stewart Crafts merchandising department. Emily lives in Brooklyn, NY.

tombyillustration.com

ILANA KOHN

Knitted Cat Toys, page 107
Marbled Scarves and Handkerchiefs, page 115

Ilana studied illustration and historic preservation at Pratt Institute. After working as an illustrator for many years, she launched her clothing line under her own name in 2010. Her collection focuses on textile prints, including one-of-a-kind marbled pieces. She strives to create clothing and accessories that are classic looking and easy to wear. She lives in Brooklyn, NY.

ilanakohn.com

SIAN KEEGAN

Sewn and Stuffed Toys, page 141
Patchwork Pillow, page 145

Originally from Connecticut, Sian moved to New York City to pursue a BFA in surface design from the Fashion Institute of Technology. She works as a freelance textile designer and a stuffed animal maker, and custom-makes her well-known dog "portraits" using all recycled fabrics. Her book, *How to Make Stuffed Animals*, was published in 2012. She lives in Brooklyn, NY.

siankeegan.com

ERIN CONSIDINE

Coiled Bowls, page 149
Woven Camera Strap, page 153

A third-generation craftsperson, Erin attended North Carolina's Penland School of Crafts. She went on to focus on metals, small-scale sculpture, and sustainability at the Evergreen State College in Olympia, Washington. After relocating to New York, she launched her jewelry line in 2009, merging her skill as a metalsmith and a lifelong passion for fiber. Erin lives in Brooklyn, NY.

erinconsidine.com

ERIN WECKERLE

Freeform Knitted Throw, page 123
Crocheted Garland, page 127

After earning a master's degree in painting at Yale, Erin started her knitwear line, Purldrop, and opened her own shop, Sodafine, which she stocked with carefully chosen, handmade, one-of-a-kind, and environmentally sustainable items. In 2011, Erin closed Sodafine to pursue new projects. She is now focusing on creating art and teaching knitting and crochet. Erin lives in Brooklyn, NY.

erinweckerle.com

SHABD SIMON-ALEXANDER

Tie-Dyed Pillowcases, page 133
Tie-Dyed Baby Blanket, page 137

Shabd moved to New York in 2000 to study photography at New York University. In 2009, she launched her eponymous fashion label, which focuses on one-of-a-kind, hand-dyed garments and blurs the lines between fashion, craft, and art. Her instructional dyeing book, *Tie-Dye: Dye It, Wear It, Share It*, will be published in 2013. She lives in Brooklyn, NY.

shabdismyname.com

THE PROJECTS

ROTARY-PRINTED CLOTH NAPKINS
WITH LENA CORWIN

While planning this book, I spent time experimenting with printing techniques that were new to me, and I became especially interested in the concept of rotary printing. When manufacturers produce rotary-printed fabric, a large cylinder is carved with impressions and is used to print on long, continuous rolls of fabric. Wondering if I could make a smaller-scale rotating stamp to print an allover pattern, I adhered foam pieces to a rolling pin, and it worked. The foam pieces soak up the ink, and the design can be rolled along fabric or paper. For this napkin project, I chose a simple scattered dot design, which I especially like printed in neon ink, but a more complex design can be used, too. One yard of fabric will make four napkins, and the newsprint used under the fabric while printing can be recycled as wrapping paper.

MATERIALS:

Apron (optional)

Metal hole punch, with ¼" (6 mm) hole or larger

¼" (6 mm)-thick foam sheet, approximately 8½" x 11" (21 cm x 27.5 cm)

Small scissors (optional)

Multisurface waterproof glue

18" (45 cm) wooden rolling pin (an even cylinder rolling pin, not tapered)

Paper cup (optional)

Small paintbrush (optional)

1 yard (1 m) muslin, for test printing

4 yards (4 m) light- or medium-weight cotton, washed, dried, and ironed

Fabric scissors

18" x 24" (45 cm x 60 cm) pad newsprint paper

Plastic artist's palette, at least 18" x 15" (45 cm x 37.5 cm)

Water-based acrylic fabric ink, in colors of your choice

Old spoon

Foam brayer

Rag or paper towel

Thread in color matching fabric

Sewing machine

A) Glue dots to rolling pin

B) Finished rotary stamps

C) Spread ink with brayer

1. SET UP: You will need a work surface of approximately 5' x 3' (1.5 m x 1 m). While water-based ink is considered nontoxic, it is best to work in a well-ventilated area. Wear an apron if you wish to protect your clothing from stray ink.

2. MAKE ROTARY STAMP: Using the hole punch, create holes in the foam sheet. Keep the small foam circles you punch out and set them aside.

Note: If you're having a hard time fitting the foam into the hole punch, try punching close to the edge of the foam, pushing back and forth. Alternatively, you can cut out any shapes you like using small scissors.

Lay the rolling pin on your work surface and carefully glue each foam dot (or other shape) to the rolling pin. You can use the glue directly from the bottle, or you can pour the glue into a paper cup and use a paintbrush to dab glue on the underside of each foam piece. Create a random pattern on the rolling pin, gluing some dots close together in clusters and others farther apart *(A)*. Allow the glue to dry before you rotate the rolling pin to add more foam dots. Continue gluing dots or shapes until the entire rolling pin is covered *(B)*. Allow the glue to dry for several hours or overnight.

3. CUT FABRIC: Either iron the muslin and napkin fabric or pull the (still warm) fabric from the dryer and press out any wrinkles with your hands. Cut both the muslin and napkin fabric into 18" (45 cm) square pieces.

4. PRINT TEST FABRIC: Place two pieces of newsprint, side by side, on your work surface. Lay the muslin test fabric on top of the newsprint, smoothing out the fabric with your hands. Place your artist's palette to one side. Open your ink and stir it. The consistency should be like melted ice cream. If the ink is too thick, add a small amount (approximately 1 teaspoon) of water and stir thoroughly. Add more if needed. If your ink is too thin, leave it uncovered and exposed to air until it thickens.

Using the spoon, scoop out approximately 2 tablespoons of ink onto the palette. Spread out the ink with the spoon, creating a line across the width of the palette. Take the foam brayer and spread the ink further, creating a rectangle of ink approximately 16" (40 cm) wide and 10" (25 cm) long *(C)*. Place the rolling pin on the ink and slowly roll the pin back and forth through the ink *(D)*. I prefer to hold the pin itself, rather than the handles, by placing my fingers between the foam dots, which

D) Roll stamp through ink   *E) Check for ink on pin*   *F) Roll pin over fabric*

gives me more control while rolling (sometimes the pin will skid along the palette instead of rolling when the handles are used).

Lift the rolling pin and stand it upright, resting the handle on your work surface. Check to see if any ink has gotten on the rolling pin, and if so, wipe those areas with a paper towel or rag *(E)*. Place the rolling pin on the edge of the test fabric and slowly roll the pin away from you *(F)*. Note that for the first rotation of the rolling pin, the ink is heavily coated on the foam and only a little pressure is needed. As you finish one rotation of the rolling pin, the printed ink will start to appear lighter, so you will need to apply increasing pressure as you approach the second rotation. With practice you will be able to achieve two rotations of the rolling pin with nice, even prints. If your print has globs of excess ink, you are pressing too hard. If your print is faded, you are pressing too lightly.

After two rotations of the rolling pin, stop to roll the foam brayer on the palette to redistribute the ink, and reapply the ink to the rolling pin. Add more ink to the palette as needed. Lay down fresh sheets of newsprint for each piece of fabric, and practice printing on the test fabric until you are happy with the appearance of your prints.

5. PRINT NAPKINS: Lay down fresh newsprint on your work surface and place a piece of napkin fabric on top. Print as you did with the test fabric, rolling the foam brayer on the palette to redistribute the ink, applying the ink to the rolling pin, and checking for stray ink. Roll the pin over the fabric, adding pressure as you finish the first rotation. Place the printed napkin fabric in a place where it can dry completely.

6. SWITCH INK COLORS: If you want to switch to a different color, wash the palette, foam brayer, and rolling pin with cold or warm water. Press the brayer and rolling pin with a rag or towel and wipe the palette to speed up the drying time. (If you want to roll a second color on the same fabric, wait until the first layer of ink is dry.) When the fabric is completely dry, iron the pieces on high heat or dry them in a machine dryer on high heat for 15 minutes. This will make the ink permanent and washable.

7. SEW NAPKINS: Hem the edges by folding the fabric under a scant ¼" (6 mm) and then a generous ¼" (6 mm) and sewing with a straight stitch in a thread color matching the fabric.

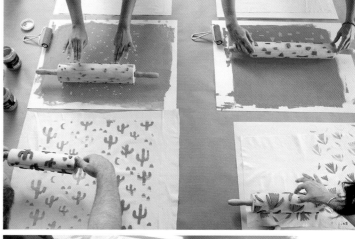

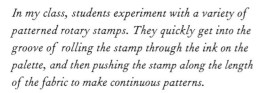

In my class, students experiment with a variety of patterned rotary stamps. They quickly get into the groove of rolling the stamp through the ink on the palette, and then pushing the stamp along the length of the fabric to make continuous patterns.

SCREEN-PRINTED
MULTICOLOR FABRIC

WITH LENA CORWIN

Screen printing can be complex enough with just one layer of ink, so in my first book, Printing by Hand, *I focused on single-color prints. But when I taught introduction to screen printing* classes at my studio, I was often asked how to print multiple colors. Traditionally, multi-colored prints (whether on paper or fabric) require taking exact measurements and making registration marks. Since I like to work in a looser way, I experimented with methods of printing several colors without the tedious process of print registration. For this project, I created several motifs on the screen using tape, so I would be able to print multiple colors at once down the length of the fabric. With this technique, the printing goes very quickly, and the screen can be used again and again. This is a more advanced printing project, and you should be comfortable with basic screen printing before trying this method. To find the large silkscreen and small squeegees I suggest, you will probably need to go to a screen-printing supply store or a well-stocked art supply store (see Resources, page 175). If you are a beginner, try following these instructions using just one color of ink instead of multiple colors and one large squeegee instead of several small squeegees.

MATERIALS:

Apron

Silk screen, approximately 18" x 24" (45 cm x 60 cm)

Artist's tape in a variety of widths, from ¼" to 2" (6 mm to 5 cm)

Scissors (use a cheap pair of scissors that you won't mind getting gummy from tape)

Paper and pencil (optional)

2½ yards (2½ m) cotton or linen fabric, washed, dried, and ironed

Fabric scissors

5 (8-ounce / 235-ml) containers of water-based fabric screen-printing ink, in colors of your choice

5 old spoons*

Small plastic containers with lids for mixing ink (optional)*

5 small squeegees, ranging in size from 3" to 6" (7.5 cm to 15 cm)

Old towel

Old blanket

Rags or paper towels

Sponge (optional)

Mild dish soap (optional)

*Not to be used again for food

A) Tape outline of shapes   *B) Fill in screen with tape*   *C) Print first motif*

1. SET UP: You will need a work surface of approximately 4' x 8' (1.2 m x 2.5 m), on a table or on the floor. Wear an apron while mixing the ink and printing. Water-based ink is considered non-toxic, but it is best to work in a well-ventilated area. Make sure you have adequate space when screen printing and keep your workspace tidy and organized so you can work quickly.

2. PLAN DESIGN: Create a design on the screen by taping the negative space around the shapes; the areas left untaped will print onto the fabric. When creating your own design with tape, shapes with mostly straight lines are easiest. You might want to sketch pattern ideas onto paper before you start taping your screen. Keep in mind that the design must include enough space between the motifs for the squeegee to spread the ink over each color without the inks touching. (See *Fig. 1* for examples of optimal spacing and layouts that would work well.) For an 18" x 24" (45 cm x 60 cm) screen, a design with three to five colors works best.

3. TAPE SCREEN: Place the screen on the work surface, mesh-side up. Begin placing tape on your screen mesh to outline the shapes in your design *(A)*. Continue placing tape until the entire negative space around your design is covered *(B)*. The tape can be repositioned over and over (until it loses stickiness), so you can continue to adjust your design as you tape. Overlap the tape strips so no ink can seep through while printing. When you have finished taping your entire design, hold the screen up to a window to see if you have accidentally left any areas untaped.

4. CUT FABRIC AND MIX INK: Cut ½ yard (½ m) from the fabric to use as test fabric. The remaining 2 yards (2 m) will be your printing fabric. If you want to mix a new color, scoop a few tablespoons of ink into a plastic container and mix it thoroughly. Always start with small amounts to avoid waste in case you do not like the color. Dab a bit of the mixed ink on the test fabric and allow it to dry to see the most accurate color. Adding a drop of black or brown will bring down the brightness of a color. The consistency should be like melted ice cream. If the ink is too thick, add a small amount (approximately 1 teaspoon) of water and stir thoroughly. Add more water as needed. If your ink is too thin, leave it uncovered and exposed to air until it thickens.

5. PREPARE TO PRINT FABRIC: Place the old towel and blanket side by side on your work surface. Place the test fabric on top of the towel and your 2 yards (2 m) of printing fabric on top of the

D) Print all motifs

E) A row of prints

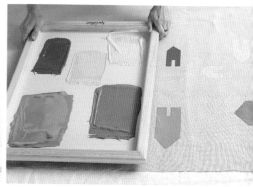

F) Set screen close to previous print without touching it

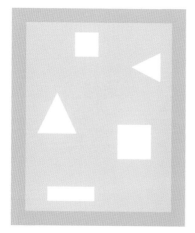

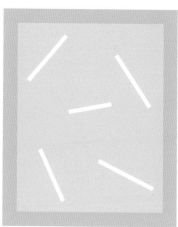

Fig. 1: Optimal motif spacing

blanket. Smooth out any wrinkles with your hands. Place the ink and squeegees on the left side of the work surface. Do a mental run-through for printing the fabric: You will begin by printing all five colors on the test fabric, and then move immediately to the 2-yard (2-m) length of fabric, where you will make 8 prints total, working from left to right (4 prints along the top of the fabric, and then 4 more prints below [*Fig. 2*]).

6. PRINT FABRIC: When you begin printing you will want to move at a quick pace so the ink does not dry in the screen. When printing with water-based ink, drying is always a concern, though it should not be a problem if you always keep the screen wet with ink and then wash the screen immediately when finished.

Place the screen mesh-side down on the test fabric. Use a spoon to scoop approximately 1 tablespoon of ink onto the screen in a line to the side of one motif. Repeat with a different color for each motif, using a different spoon for each color. Take one of the squeegees and pass it across one motif at a 45-degree angle *(C)*, dragging the line of ink and applying pressure as you pull. Pick up the squeegee, turn it around, and pull it back in the other direction. Repeat. Next, drag the squeegee over the motif once more without applying pressure—this will keep the screen wet and prevent the ink from drying in the mesh. Set the squeegee down to the left of the fabric. Use a new squeegee to print each motif in the design *(D)*. Rest the wet squeegees to the left of your fabric. Then, lift the screen by pulling it up from the front at a 45-degree angle *(E)*. If the print looks good, move on to the fabric yardage. If not, continue "warming up" the screen by making test prints.

25

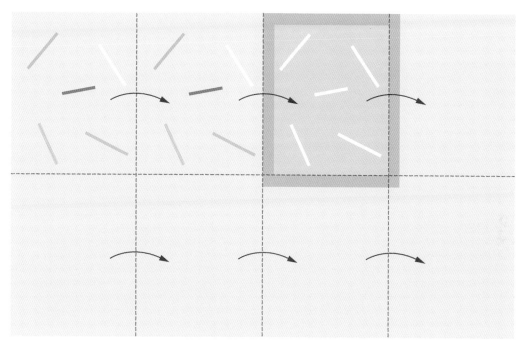

Fig. 2: Begin printing at top left and print across top row

Start printing on the fabric yardage by placing the screen, mesh-side down, on the fabric at the top left *(Fig. 2)*. Print as you did for the test fabric. Lift the screen and set it down again to the right of the first print, as close to the first print as possible without touching any wet ink *(F)*. Repeat twice more along the top of the fabric for a total of 4 prints, then make 4 prints along the bottom of the fabric.

7. WASH SCREEN: When the last print is complete, carefully scrape the extra ink off the screen and squeegees and back into their respective ink containers (if the colors have mixed on the screen, store the mixed ink in a separate airtight container). Wash the screen, squeegees, and spoons with cold or warm water in a large sink or bathtub. A sponge and mild dish soap can be used. Peel off all the tape and discard it. Make sure to wash the screen very well—you can hold the screen up to a light to see if any ink is remaining in the mesh. You might see a haze of color left on your screen, which is fine.

8. FINISH: Allow the printed fabric to dry completely. To heat set the fabric (making it permanent and washable), place it in the dryer on high heat for 15 minutes.

SEWN DRESS AND TOP

WITH JENNY GORDY

While Jenny honed her sewing skills in fashion school, she was originally taught to sew by her grandmother (after whom her company, Wiksten, is named), and in recent years she has begun selling original sewing patterns. The inspiration for this pattern comes from the thrifty idea of making a child's dress out of an old pillowcase, though pillowcases are too small for the grown-up version. This versatile and adjustable style can be made in three lengths—a top, a short dress, or a long dress with a drawstring waist. In these instructions, Jenny shows you how to draft a pattern tailored to your measurements, and then how to sew it together in the fabric of your choice. It may sound complex, but it is actually quite simple and is a great "beginner" project for those who have never made a garment before. Jenny always had great tips for students in her classes, like encouraging them to use an edge-stitching foot and a seam gauge—both of which help make the finished product look polished—and Jenny includes lots of great tips in this project, too.

MATERIALS:

Measuring tape

Paper for the pattern (butcher paper, tracing paper, or newsprint all work well):

- 2 pieces of 24" x 30" (60 cm x 75 cm) paper for top
- 2 pieces of 24" x 36" (60 cm x 90 cm) paper for short dress
- 2 pieces of 24" x 50" (60 cm x 125 cm) paper for long dress

Pencil

Paper scissors

Ruler

Iron

Straight pins

Lightweight fabric (such as cotton, linen, or silk), washed, dried, and ironed:

- 1½ yards (1½ m) for top
- 2 yards (2 m) for short dress
- 2¼ yards (2¼ m) for long dress

Fabric scissors

Sewing machine

Matching thread

Large safety pin

Seam gauge

Tailor's chalk, disappearing-ink pen, or needle and thread for marking the pattern (needed only if adding the drawstring waist to the dress)

A) Use iron to draft armhole

B) Use iron to draft neckline

C) Check that pattern piece is on grain

1. TAKE MEASUREMENTS AND DRAFT PATTERN: Use the measuring tape to measure your hip and waist circumferences *(Fig. 1)*; write these numbers down. To find out the hip width needed for your pattern piece, add 10" (25 cm) to your hip circumference measurement, and then divide that number by 4.

Look at *Fig. 2* to find out the measurements for the garment length (depending on if you want to make a top, short dress, or long dress), as well as for the neckline and armhole. (Note that these measurements include seam allowances.)

Using these measurements and *Fig. 2* as a guide, draft a to-scale body pattern on paper with pencil. To create the curve of the armhole and neckline on your body pattern piece, trace around the curve of your (completely cool) iron *(A + B)*. Using *Fig. 3* as a guide, draft a to-scale shoulder-strap pattern piece.

If you want a more defined silhouette, it's easy to make a drawstring waist (either at your natural waist or higher for an empire waist (which makes the dress a great maternity piece). To draft a pattern for a waistline, draft and cut out the drawstring and the drawstring casing pattern pieces using these measurements:

Drawstring length: Your waist circumference + 20" (50 cm) = _____" / cm
Drawstring width: 1½" (4 cm)

Drawstring casing length = Your hip circumference + 8" (20 cm) = _____" / cm
Drawstring casing width = 1" (2.5 cm)

When your body, strap, and drawstring patterns are drafted, cut out the patterns with paper scissors.

2. CUT FABRIC: You will be cutting the following pieces from the fabric: 2 body pieces, each cut on the fold; 2 shoulder straps; 1 drawstring and 1 drawstring casing (optional).

Fold the fabric in half, with wrong sides facing and the selvedges together, and place it on your work surface. The body you drafted will need to be cut out on the fold of the fabric twice, since the front and back are the same. The other pieces do not need to be cut on the fold, but they do need to be cut along the grain of the fabric (you can use a ruler to make sure your pattern pieces are straight along the grain) *(C)*. Pin the pattern pieces to the fabric *(D)*, and cut the pieces out *(E)*.

D) Pin pattern piece to fabric

E) Cut out pieces

F) Press ½" (12 mm) to wrong side

Fig. 1: Body measurements

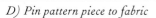

waist circumference

hip circumference

Fig. 2: Body pattern piece measurements

2½" (6.5 cm)

1" (2.5 cm)

6½" (16.5 cm)

long dress length: 40" (1 m)

short dress length: 34" (85 cm)

top length: 23" (57.5 cm)

FOLD

TOP HEM

SHORT DRESS HEM

LONG DRESS HEM

(hip + 10"/25 cm) ÷ 4

Fig. 3: Shoulder strap and drawstring measurements

30" (75 cm)

SHOULDER STRAP X2

1½" (4 cm)

waist circumference + 20" (50 cm)

OPTIONAL DRAWSTRING

1½" (4 cm)

hip circumference + 8" (20 cm)

OPTIONAL DRAWSTRING CASING

1" (2.5 cm)

G) Tuck in raw edge   H) Edge-stitch neckline   I) Encased seam

3. SEW ARMHOLE SEAM: Press armholes ½" (12 mm) to the wrong side *(F)*, then tuck the raw edges under to meet the fold *(G)*, pressing and pinning as you go. The armhole hem will be ¼" (6 mm) wide. Edge-stitch the fold, backtacking at the beginning and end.

4. SEW NECKLINE CASING: Press the neckline on the front and back ¾" (16 mm) to the wrong side, then tuck the raw edges under so the neck casing is ½" (12 mm) wide, pressing and pinning as you go (make sure the side edges of the neckline are tucked in neatly). Edge-stitch the fold *(H)* to create a casing for the shoulder strap, backtacking at the beginning and end.

5. SEW SIDE SEAMS: Pin the front and back body pieces together at the side seams, with wrong sides facing. Sew both sides with ¼" (6 mm) seams, backtacking at the beginning and end, and press the seams open. Trim the seams to ⅛" (3 mm). Turn the garment inside out, and press the side seams. Sew a second seam ¼" (6 mm) from the pressed folded seam, so that you are encasing the previous seam allowance (this type of seam is known as a French seam; *Fig. 4*). Backtack at the beginning and end, and press the seams to one side *(I + J)*.

6. SEW HEM: With the garment still inside out, press the hem 1" (2.5 cm) to the wrong side, then tuck the raw edge under to meet the fold, pressing and pinning as you go. The hem will be ½" (12 mm) wide. Edge-stitch the hem, backtacking at the beginning and end.

7. SEW SHOULDER STRAPS AND DRAWSTRING: Press the short ends of the shoulder strap ½" (12 mm) to the wrong side. Fold and press the strap in half lengthwise, wrong sides together, to find the middle. Fold both long edges in to meet the middle crease and press. Fold the strap in half along the middle crease and edge-stitch along the length of the strap, backtacking at the beginning and end *(Fig. 5)*. Repeat with the other shoulder strap. If you are including a drawstring, sew it the same way as you sewed the straps. Attach a safety pin to one end of each shoulder strap and thread a strap through each neckline casing *(K + L)*. Remove the safety pin and knot the ends of the straps above the shoulders.

8. SEW OPTIONAL DRAWSTRING WAIST: Try on the top/dress and mark the line on the body where the drawstring casing will be sewn, using either tailor's chalk or a disappearing-ink pen, or by

J) Finished French seam   *K) Thread strap through casing*   *L) Pull strap through casing*

basting with thread. (For an empire waist, mark 2" [5 cm] above the waistline.) Make sure the waist is parallel to the hem all the way around. For the casing, fold the short ends ½" (12 mm) to the wrong side and press. Then press the long, raw edges ¼" (6 mm) to the wrong side, so the casing is ½" (12 mm) wide. Pin the casing to the dress and edge-stitch in place, leaving a 1" (2.5 cm) gap between the casing ends at the center front of the dress. Attach a safety pin to the end of the draw-string and thread it through the casing. Remove the pin and knot each end of the drawstring.

Fig. 4: French seam   *Fig. 5: Sewing straps*

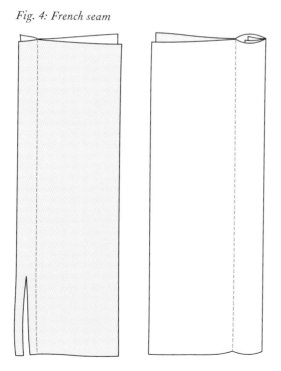

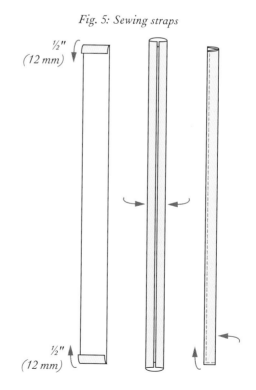

½"
(12 mm)

½"
(12 mm)

KNITTED SOCKS

WITH JENNY GORDY

When Jenny taught sewing classes in my studio, people were always quick to sign up. I think part of the popularity of her classes was due to her signature style—particularly the colors and materials she chooses—and her attention to detail. Jenny applies this same sense of style to the knitwear she designs. I always wanted her to teach a sock-knitting class, but we weren't able to make it happen before she moved away from New York City. Before she left, however, she did walk me through the steps for knitting a baby sweater. Like many people, I only had basic knitting skills and had never made anything more challenging than a scarf—plus I've always been a bit intimidated by the shorthand used in most knitting patterns. I was struck by how much less intimidating the pattern was when she "translated" the instructions for me into plain English (and how patient she was to do that). Jenny wrote out the instructions for these socks in the same way. Whether you make the boot sock or ankle sock, we hope that these spelled-out instructions give you confidence to give knitting "beyond the scarf" a try, even if you're just a beginner.

SIZES
Women's sizes 6 (7, 8, 9, 10)

FINISHED MEASUREMENTS
8" (20 cm) Foot and Leg circumference

Leg length from top of Cuff to base of Heel: 10" (25 cm) for boot socks; 4" (10 cm) for ankle socks

8¼ (8¾, 9¼ , 9¾, 10¼)" [21 (22, 23.5, 25, 26) cm] Foot length from back of Heel to end of Toe

YARN

VARIEGATED BOOT SOCKS:
Koigu Painter's Palette Premium Merino (KPPPM) (100% merino wool; 175 yards / 160 m; 50 grams): 2 hanks #P465 (A)

CONTRAST CUFF ANKLE SOCKS:
Anzula Squishy (80% superwash merino / 10% cashmere / 10% nylon; 385 yards / 352 m; 115 grams): 1 hank each Clay (B) and Persimmon (C)

NEEDLES
One set of five double-pointed needles size US 2 (2.75 mm) (change needle size if necessary to obtain correct gauge)

NOTIONS
Stitch marker (optional)
Tapestry needle

GAUGE
30 stitches and 40 rows = 4" (10 cm) in Stockinette stitch

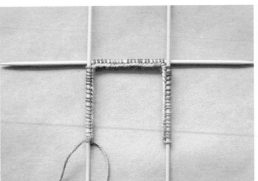

A) Cast on stitches   *B) Divide stitches onto 3 needles*   *C) Join stitches in the round*

1. KNIT CUFF: *(Note: See page 169 for a knitting basics tutorial.)*

Cast on 60 stitches using color A or C, depending on which sock you're knitting, and the Long-Tail Cast-On method (see page 169) *(A)*.

Move the first 20 stitches onto a second needle, then move the next 20 stitches onto a third needle. Your stitches are now divided evenly among three needles *(B)*.

Rotate your knitting so the tail is on the right side. Make sure that none of your stitches are twisted as you slip a fourth needle into the first stitch on the left side *(C)*. Knit into this first stitch using the yarn attached to the needle on the right, pulling tightly to avoid gapping.

Your knitting is now joined in the round, and you will continue to work in rounds. When you reach the beginning of each needle, scoot your work to the tip of the needle closest to you and use your hands just as if you were knitting with only 2 needles (one with stitches in your left hand, and an empty needle in your right hand), ignoring the other 2 needles. Knit the stitches onto the empty needle. When finished, push the stitches back to the middle of the needle and move on to the next one.

Place a marker on the first stitch to indicate the beginning of the round (or simply use the hanging tail as your guide). Go on and knit the second stitch. Purl the next 2 stitches. Repeat this knit 2, purl 2 rib pattern until your Cuff measures 2" (5 cm) long for boot socks or 1" (2.5 cm) long for ankle socks, stopping at the end of a round *(D)*.

2. KNIT LEG: (Change to color B if you're working Contrast Cuff Ankle Socks.) Work in Stockinette stitch, knitting every round until your work measures 8" (20 cm) from the top of the Cuff for boot socks, or 2" (5 cm) from the top of the Cuff for ankle socks. Stop at the end of a round.

3. KNIT HEEL FLAP: To divide stitches for the Heel Flap, slip the last 15 stitches of the round onto your fourth needle, then also knit the next 15 stitches in the round onto that needle (30 stitches on the fourth needle). You will now continue to work back and forth with only the 30 stitches on this needle for the Heel Flap. Place the remaining stitches onto 1 needle for the top of the Foot. Your stitches are now divided evenly onto 2 needles.

ROW 1 (WRONG SIDE): Starting on the wrong side, slip 1 stitch purlwise with yarn held to the front, purl 29.

D) Ribbed cuff

E) Heel flap

F) Turning the heel

*G) Pick up and knit stitches
along sides of heel flap*

H) 84 stitches on 3 needles

I) Knit foot

ROW 2 (RIGHT SIDE): Slip 1 stitch purlwise with yarn held to the back, knit 1; repeat slip 1 purlwise, knit 1 pattern across the row.
Repeat Rows 1 and 2 until Heel Flap is 2¼" (5.5 cm) long, ending with a right-side row *(E)*.

4. TURN HEEL: *ROW 1 (WRONG SIDE):* Slip 1 stitch purlwise, purl 16, purl 2 together, purl 1. Turn your work to the right side.
ROW 2: Slip 1 purlwise, knit 5, slip 1 knitwise, knit 1, pass slipped stitch over, knit 1. Turn.
ROW 3: Slip 1 purlwise, purl 6, purl 2 together, purl 1. Turn.
ROW 4: Slip 1 purlwise, knit 7, slip 1 knitwise, knit 1, pass slipped stitch over, knit 1. Turn.
ROW 5: Slip 1 purlwise, purl 8, purl 2 together, purl 1. Turn.
ROW 6: Slip 1 purlwise, knit 9, slip 1 knitwise, knit 1, pass slipped stitch over, knit 1. Turn.
ROW 7: Slip 1 purlwise, purl 10, purl 2 together, purl 1. Turn.
ROW 8: Slip 1 purlwise, knit 11, slip 1 knitwise, knit 1, pass slipped stitch over, knit 1. Turn.
ROW 9: Slip 1 purlwise, purl 12, purl 2 together, purl 1. Turn.
ROW 10: Slip 1 purlwise, knit 13, slip 1 knitwise, knit 1, pass slipped stitch over, knit 1. Turn.
ROW 11: Slip 1 purlwise, purl 14, purl 2 together, purl 1. Turn.
ROW 12: Slip 1 purlwise, knit 15, slip 1 knitwise, knit 1, pass slipped stitch over, knit 1. Turn.
You will have 18 stitches remaining on your Heel needle *(F)*.

J) Thread tail through live stitches *K) Cinch toe closed* *L) Cast on for your second sock*

5. KNIT GUSSET: You will now pick up stitches and reincorporate the top-of-Foot stitches into working in rounds again.

RIGHT SIDE: Use a third needle to pick up and knit 18 stitches along the left side of the Heel Flap. Knit the 30 stitches across the top of the Foot onto another needle. With a fourth needle, pick up and knit 18 stitches along the other side of the Heel Flap *(G)*. Knit the first 9 stitches from the Heel needle onto the needle with which you just picked up stitches. Slip the remaining 9 Heel stitches onto the next needle. You now have 84 stitches on 3 needles (27 stitches on first needle, 30 on second, and 27 on third) *(H)*.

Begin working in rounds.
ROUND 1: FIRST NEEDLE: Knit to last 2 stitches on needle, knit 2 together. SECOND NEEDLE: Knit all 30 stitches across top of Foot. THIRD NEEDLE: Slip 1 knitwise, knit 1, pass slipped stitch over, knit to end of round.
ROUND 2: Knit all stitches.
Repeat Rounds 1 and 2 until you have 60 stitches total (15 stitches on first needle, 30 on second, 15 on third).

6. KNIT FOOT: Knit all rounds *(I)* until Foot measures 6 (6½, 7, 7½, 8)" [15 (16.5, 18, 19, 20) cm] from back edge of Heel.

7. KNIT TOE: Begin decreasing to shape Toe.
ROUND 1: FIRST NEEDLE: Knit to last 2 stitches, knit 2 together. SECOND NEEDLE: Slip 1 knitwise, knit 1, pass slipped stitch over, knit to last 2 stitches, knit 2 together. THIRD NEEDLE: Slip 1 knitwise, knit 1, pass slipped stitch over, knit to end of round.
ROUNDS 2–4: Knit all stitches. Repeat Rounds 1–4 two more times—48 stitches remain.
Starting here, every round will be a decrease round. Repeat Round 1 until 12 stitches remain.

Cut a nice long tail. Using a tapestry needle, thread the tail through the last 12 stitches *(J)* and cinch the end of the Toe closed *(K)*. Pull tight to avoid a hole, and weave in ends. Cast on for your second sock *(L)* and repeat steps 1–7.

TEA-DYED APPLIQUÉ CROSS PILLOW
WITH LIANE TYRREL

The first time I saw Liane's work was at a friend's studio, where I was drawn to a small, stone-gray pillow she had appliquéd with a cross and filled with buckwheat hulls. I've always found the soft, worn-in look of over-dyed fabrics really appealing. Liane began experimenting with natural and foraged dye materials when she started her home goods company, Enhabiten, in 2008. In order to achieve one of her favorite grays, she first dyes fabric with foraged sumac leaves and then over-dyes with iron from rusty nails. Tea dyeing is a great, easy way to begin experimenting with natural plant pigments, and using black tea yields a variety of earthy shades, from off-white to pinky brown. The dyed fabric is fairly colorfast and can be washed and dried, though repeated laundering or sustained exposure to the sun may cause slight fading. The wool and cotton fabrics used in this project take tea staining beautifully, as would other natural fibers.

MATERIALS:

Large cooking pot

Black tea bags, any variety

1 yard (1 m) white felted wool for the cover and sample strips

¼ yard (¼ m) cotton sheeting for the appliqué and sample strips

Fabric scissors

Large wooden or metal spoon

Old towel

Measuring tape

Tracing paper

Paper scissors

Pencil

Liquid castile soap

Straight pins

Fabric spray temporary adhesive (optional)

Hand-sewing needle

Sewing machine (optional)

Off-white thread

1 yard (1 m) muslin for the pillow insert

Stuffing, such as kapok
(see Resources, page 175)

Paper dust mask (optional)

Lint brush or packing tape

A) Remove tea bags

B) Test tea stain shades

C) Cut out template

1. PREPARE TEA BATH: Fill a large pot about three-quarters full with water. Bring the water to a boil over high heat, then drop in 8 to 10 tea bags and stir. Turn the heat down to a simmer and allow the bags to steep for 5 to 10 minutes. Remove the bags from the liquid and discard *(A)*. Keep the tea simmering.

2. TEST TEA STAIN: Cut a 1" x 9" (2.5 cm x 22.5 cm) strip from both the felted wool and cotton sheeting and cut each strip into 3 pieces. Place one sample piece of each fabric in the pot while the tea is simmering. Use a spoon to submerge the pieces and stir them around, allowing the fabrics to absorb the liquid. It will take just a few minutes for the fabric to turn a rich brown when the tea is hot. To achieve lighter shades, remove the tea from the heat and allow the liquid to cool before adding your other test fabric pieces. Submerge the pieces and stir them around. Take them out when the desired shades are achieved. Lay the strips on an old towel to dry, and make a record of how you achieved each shade, how long each sample piece was in the tea bath, and whether the liquid was hot or cool *(B)*.

3. CUT AND DYE PILLOW FABRIC: Lay a piece of tracing paper over the cross template on page 167, and trace over the shape with a pencil. Using paper scissors, cut out the shape from the tracing paper *(C)*. Lay the wool out on a flat surface. Using the measuring tape and pencil, measure and mark two 13" (32.5 cm) square pieces of wool, then cut them out with fabric scissors. Cut a square of the cotton slightly larger than the cross template. (You will dye this piece prior to cutting out the cross.)

Submerge your pillow pieces and cross fabric piece in the tea bath *(D)*, using the test pieces and your notes to achieve the desired shade. Dye the body fabric and cross fabric the same shade, or vary the timing and temperature of the tea bath to create different shades.

Once the fabrics are tea-stained, lay them out flat on an old towel to dry and allow the stain to set. Once they are dry, handwash them with cool water and castile soap to rinse out any excess tea. Lay the fabric flat on an old towel to dry.

When the dyed cotton fabric is dry, pin the cross pattern to the fabric with straight pins, and cut out the cross *(E)*.

| D) Stain fabric | E) Cut out cross | F) Sew cross to pillow top |

4. SEW PILLOW: Fold one of the wool pieces into quarters to find the center. Unfold the wool and place the cross in the center. If desired, apply a coat of fabric adhesive to the back of your cross piece and reposition the cross on the wool. (The adhesive will help keep the cross in place as you sew.) Using a needle and off-white thread, hand-sew the cross to the pillow top with a rustic stitch *(F)*.

Lay the top and bottom pillow fabric pieces with right sides together and the edges aligned, and pin the corners. Using a sewing machine (or tight hand stitches), sew around the edges with a ⅝" (15 mm) seam allowance, leaving a 4" (10 cm) opening for the pillow insert. Turn the pillow cover right-side out and iron lightly.

5. SEW PILLOW INSERT AND FINISH PILLOW: Lay the muslin on a flat surface. Using the measuring tape and pencil, measure and mark two 13" (32.5 cm) square pieces of muslin and cut them out with fabric scissors. Lay the pieces with right sides together and the edges aligned and pin the corners. Using a sewing machine (or tight hand stitches), sew the edges with a ⅝" (15 mm) seam allowance, leaving a 4" (10 cm) opening for stuffing the insert. Turn the fabric right-side out.

Stuff the muslin pillow insert with stuffing or kapok to the desired firmness (you may want to wear a dust mask while handling the stuffing), then hand-stitch the opening of the pillow insert closed. Use a lint brush or a length of packing tape to remove any filling stuck to the surface of your pillow insert. Place the pillow insert inside the pillow cover and hand-stitch the opening closed.

To wash the pillow, spot clean or wash on the "delicate" or "handwash" setting of your washing machine, and air dry.

OLIVE OIL SOAP

WITH LIANE TYRREL

Soap made with 100 percent olive oil (also called castile soap) is a very gentle cleanser with a smooth and creamy lather, and it is great for all skin types, particularly sensitive skin. The soap-making technique demonstrated here is called cold process; lye and oil are mixed together to create a chemical reaction called saponification, and the end result is soap. When Liane began making soap, she was working full-time at an art gallery and craved projects that required using her hands. After following a basic soap recipe like this one many times, she started to experiment with adding other ingredients, like lemon or eucalyptus oil. She suggests that new soap makers do the same.

Note: Always use caution when working with lye (sodium hydroxide) because it is very caustic. Lye is corrosive to skin and other reactive surfaces, but when handled with care, it is not difficult to use. (And don't worry—when the saponification process is complete, there is no lye in the soap.)

MATERIALS:

Newsprint or drop cloth

Hot plate or stovetop

Rubber gloves

Safety goggles

Old rag

Vapor-resistant face mask (optional)

White or cider vinegar

1-pound (455-g) container of lye (sodium hydroxide)

Food or postage scale*

18-ounce (535-ml) or larger plastic container*

16-ounce (480-ml) liquid measuring cup*

2-quart (2-L) stainless steel or heat-resistant glass bowl*

10-ounce (300-ml) or larger plastic container*

2 wooden spoons or silicon spatulas*

2 candy thermometers*

½-gallon (2-L) container of 100% olive oil (not "light" or "extra-virgin")

3-quart (3-L) stainless steel or heat resistant glass cooking pot*

Immersion ("stick") blender*

6-quart (6-L) plastic food storage container, approximately 4" x 8" x 12" (10 cm x 20 cm x 30 cm), with lid*

Freezer paper

2 old towels

Chef's knife

Wire rack or wax paper

Distilled water

*Not to be used again for food

A) Pour water into larger container   *B) Pour lye into smaller container*   *C) Measure olive oil*

1. SET UP AND SAFETY: You will need a work surface at least 3' x 4' (1 m x 1.2 m). Cover your work area with newsprint or a drop cloth. You will need to heat the olive oil on a stovetop or hot plate. Read all the instructions and assemble all the ingredients and equipment before starting. Always wear rubber gloves and safety goggles when handling lye, and have an old rag handy for cleanup. Strong fumes are created when the lye is first dissolved in water. Prepare the mixture near an open window or exhaust fan, in a room away from children and pets. To avoid inhaling the fumes, hold your breath during the initial mixing and then leave the room while the air clears, or wear a vapor-resistant face mask as an extra precaution (regular dust masks are not effective). Avoid carrying an opened jug or a bowl of lye mixture—choose one spot, inside or outside, for soap making.

Never use the soap-making equipment (pots, pans, and utensils) for food preparation afterward. Clearly mark the lye container, close the lid tightly, and store it in an area away from children and pets when you've finished making soap. If you spill lye on your skin, quickly rinse it with vinegar to neutralize the lye, and then flush with warm water. Thoroughly clean your work area after using lye.

2. MIX LYE AND WATER: Place the larger plastic container on the scale and tare (zero out) the scale. Pour 16 ounces (455 g) of room-temperature water into the container *(A)*. Pour the water into the 2-quart (2-L) stainless steel or heat-resistant glass bowl. Place the smaller plastic container on the scale and tare the scale. Put on gloves and goggles, and carefully pour 7 ounces (200 g) of lye into the plastic container *(B)*. Carefully add the lye to the water. Never pour the water into the lye as this can cause a chemical reaction that would be dangerous and messy. Hold your breath and use a spoon or spatula to carefully mix the lye and water.

Leave the room for 10 minutes to allow the air to clear of lye fumes. Return and stir the mixture again, making sure that all the lye is dissolved. A chemical reaction will cause the mixture to heat up and then cool again. Place a candy thermometer in the mixture; it will not be ready to combine with the olive oil until the temperature drops to 100°F (38°C).

D) Pour oil into second pot

E) Pour lye mixture into oil and stir

F) Blend for 30 seconds

3. COMBINE LYE MIXTURE AND OLIVE OIL: Dry the measuring cup used for measuring the water. While the lye mixture is cooling, measure 50 ounces (1.42 kg) of olive oil on the scale *(C)* and pour it into the 3-quart (3-L) stainless steel or heat-resistant glass cooking pot *(D)*. Heat the oil gently on the stovetop or hot plate and track the temperature with the second candy thermometer until the oil reaches 100°F (38°C). When both the olive oil and the lye mixture are near 100°F (38°C), it is time to combine them. Wearing the gloves and goggles, carefully pour the lye mixture into the oil and stir *(E)*. Combine them using the immersion blender for approximately 30 seconds *(F)*. Next, use the blender (without the motor on) to stir the mixture for an additional 30 seconds. Take the spoon or spatula and scrape the sides to make sure all of the lye and oil are incorporated. Continue alternating between 30 seconds of blending and 30 seconds of stirring; the liquid will begin to turn cloudy and thicken.

Stop blending when the mixture has the consistency of thin pudding. When you lift the blender or spoon out of the liquid, the drips should make a pattern or "trace" on the surface. The puddinglike mixture should be very uniform in color and consistency. This mixing process generally takes 5 to 10 minutes.

4. PREPARE CONTAINER AND POUR SOAP MIXTURE: Line the 6-quart (6-L) plastic food storage container on all sides with freezer paper to prevent the soap from sticking. Pour the soap mixture into the plastic container *(G)* and close the lid. Place the container on top of one towel and wrap it on all sides. Lay a second towel on top, drape it over all sides, and tuck the towel under, making sure to keep the container level *(H)*. Set the container and towels aside in a safe, cool place.

5. CLEAN UP: Wearing the gloves and goggles, fold up the newsprint and throw it out or machine-wash the drop cloth. Wipe down your work area with a damp cloth, going over it several times. Be meticulous about cleaning up any spilled granules of lye on your work surface. Clean the containers used for mixing lye in a bucket with soap and water, not in your kitchen sink. Label the containers and save them for future soap making.

G) Pour soap mixture into container

H) Wrap container with towels

I) Cut soap into bars

6. COOL SOAP MIXTURE: After 12 to 24 hours have passed, open the soap container and take a peek. You should find a fairly hard block of soap. Cover it back up for a day or two, until the plastic container is no longer hot but still feels warm to the touch.

7. REMOVE AND CUT SOAP: Remove the block of soap from the mold by slipping a knife between the container and the soap to loosen it (you may need to hit the bottom of the container with your hand as well). Slide the block of soap onto your work surface and cut the soap into smaller bars *(I)*. Arrange the bars on a wire rack or piece of wax paper with space between each bar for air circulation.

8. FINISH: Handmade soap takes time to fully harden and for the pH level to drop. Leave the soap on the racks or wax paper for 3 to 6 weeks, turning the bars occasionally to allow airflow around all edges. It's very unlikely that any caustic lye could be left in your finished soap, but if you made an error measuring your ingredients, it is possible. If you want to test the pH level of your soap before 8 weeks, use one of these methods:

Traditional "Tongue Test": Soap makers will just barely tap the tip of their tongue to a fresh bar of soap. An electric zing, as if touching your tongue to a battery, indicates that there is lye in the soap; this soap is not safe to use.

pH Test Strips: Soap makers who don't want to do a tongue test use pH testing strips, which can be purchased at hardware stores. The strip can detect the pH of a drop of water placed on fresh soap. Lye has a pH level of 14 and finished soap should be in the range of 7 to 10.

HAND-PAINTED CHILDREN'S LEGGINGS

WITH CAITLIN MOCIUN

These colorful, banded bottoms are a miniature version of the women's leggings from a past collection of Caitlin's clothing line, Mociun. To make the original, adult version, Caitlin screen-printed jersey fabric with a pattern of dark lines; then, after she sewed the fabric into leggings, she hand-painted the colored stripes using watered-down silkscreen ink. To make this project easier, we suggest starting with presewn children's leggings that are a blend of cotton with 5 to 10 percent Lycra (since the ink bleeds too much when painting on 100-percent cotton leggings). While the steps are not complex, this project does take some time to complete because the leggings are painted in stages and the ink needs to dry completely between steps. It is best to do this project over a weekend or several days—one part can be done in the morning and then left to dry all day, and then another part done in the evening so it can dry overnight. If you know you'll want two or more pairs of leggings, we suggest working on them simultaneously.

MATERIALS:

Child's leggings (cotton/Lycra blend)

Piece of cardboard, as large as the leggings and with no creases

Pencil

Cutting mat

Razor blade or utility knife

Plastic wrap

Straight pins

Ruler

Water-soluble (disappearing-ink) fabric pen

Measuring spoons*

8-ounce (225-g) jars fabric silk screen ink, in red, yellow, blue, black, and white

Thick paper or plastic cups

Old towel

Old white T-shirt for test painting

5 to 10 old spoons*

Round-tip paintbrush, approximately $1/8$" to $1/4$" (3 mm to 6 mm)

Bag of large rubber bands

5 soft-bristle flat-tip brushes, approximately $1/2$" to $3/4$" (12 mm to 19 mm)

Paper towels

*Not to be used again for food

A) Wrap insert with plastic   *B) Draw lines on leggings*   *C) Paint lines on leg*

1. MAKE LEG INSERTS: To keep the fabric taut and prevent the ink from bleeding through to the other side of the leggings as you paint, you will need to make one cardboard leg insert. Fold the leggings in half, leg to leg, and place them on the cardboard. Trace around the perimeter of the folded legging with a pencil. The traced line around the leg might be a little larger than the actual legging, which is fine since you want the cardboard to stretch the legging a little bit when it is inserted. Place the cardboard leg on the cutting mat and cut it out using the razor blade or utility knife.

Cut a piece of plastic wrap a little longer than the cardboard and place it on your work surface. Fold the edges over so the plastic wrap is tight around all sides of the cardboard, smoothing it out as much as you can (it's okay if it's not perfectly smooth). Turn the leg to the other side and repeat with a second piece of plastic wrap *(A)*.

Slide the insert into one of the leggings' legs. Adjust the leggings so that the leg and crotch seams line up with the edges of the cardboard, and the leg opening matches up with the bottom of the cardboard leg. Use straight pins to pin the legging in place.

2. PREPARE TO PAINT LINES: Using the ruler and water-soluble pen, draw lines on the front and back of each leg *(B)*, creating guides for painting the stripes. You can look at the leggings on page 54 as a loose reference for placing the stripes.

3. MIX BROWN INK: Brown ink is a mix of yellow, red, and black silkscreen ink. Start by adding 1 tablespoon of yellow, 1 teaspoon of red, and 1 teaspoon of black to a paper or plastic cup. Stir thoroughly to combine. Add more color until you have a shade of brown to your liking. The ink should be the consistency of melted ice cream. If it is thicker, add a little water and stir thoroughly. Add more water if necessary until the desired texture is reached.

4. PAINT LINES: Lay the old towel on your work surface and place the T-shirt on the towel. With a spoon, scoop approximately 2 tablespoons of brown ink into a paper cup. Using the small round-tip paintbrush, practice painting lines on the T-shirt. Short strokes work better than dragging the paintbrush for a long distance along the fabric. Dip the brush into the ink often, picking up a small amount of ink each time. Practice thicker and thinner lines, and decide which look you prefer.

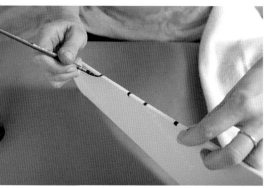

D) Paint lines on edges   *E) Switch insert to other leg*   *F) Water down the ink*

When you are happy with your brushstrokes, place the leggings on the towel and begin to paint stripes on the entire front side of the leg with the insert. Do your best to keep the leg you are not working on out of the way as you paint (you might want to cover it with part of the old towel) *(C)*. Leave it to dry thoroughly, at least several hours (you can also speed up drying with a fan or hair dryer). When the ink is completely dry, double check that there is no wet ink on the table and flip over the leggings. Paint the back side of the legging as you did the front. Make sure to paint the lines along the thin outer edges, too *(D)*. If you paint diagonal lines, pay close attention to where the stripes reach the inseam; they do not need to line up but make sure to carefully paint right up to the seam. Leave the leggings to dry thoroughly. When they are dry, switch the cardboard insert to the other leg and repeat the painting process *(E)*.

Note: While waiting for the painted lines to dry, always cover your cup of ink with a lid (or square of plastic wrap and a rubber band) so it doesn't dry out. If you need to clear your work surface, you can carefully move the leggings to dry flat elsewhere—just make sure not to smear the ink as you move them.

When all of the lines are painted and the leggings are completely dry, remove the insert and set the ink by drying the leggings in the dryer on high heat for 30 minutes. It is important not to skip this step; otherwise the brown ink will run when the colored ink is applied.

5. MIX COLORED INK: While the leggings are in the dryer, mix the colors you would like to paint between the brown lines. The inks will need to be watered down to the consistency of watercolors, but keep in mind that even though the color is watered down it will still be very vibrant. If you want light, pastel tones you will need to mix the colored ink with white ink. For a more muted color, mix in black. You can mix any color desired using the primary colors—red, yellow, and blue—plus black and white. Mix the ink thoroughly.

Add water to the cup so that the ratio of water to ink is approximately one-third water to two-thirds ink *(F)*. The texture of the watered-down ink should be similar to whole milk. Test paint the mixed colors on the T-shirt, and adjust the colors and consistency by adding more ink and/or water. Cover each cup to keep the ink from drying out.

G) Paint front and back

H) Paint first colored band

I) Paint second band

6. PAINT COLORED BANDS: Before laying out the leggings on the work surface, make sure the towel is clean. Place the cardboard insert into one leg. This time, each leg is painted in one session, front and back, by pivoting the leg as you paint *(G)*. (You can paint both the front and the back at the same time because the watered-down ink goes on like a wash, and very little ink, if any, will get on the towel.) Cover the leg that is not being painted with part of the towel.

Dip a flat-tip brush into a cup of ink and brush the ink between the leg opening and the first brown line *(H)*. If there appears to be too much ink on the fabric, blot the area with a folded paper towel. Blotting will also make the color less saturated and will keep the colors from bleeding into each other.

Carefully pivot the leg to continue painting the colored band on the back side. Make sure to paint the ¼" (6 mm) edges between the front and back.

Choose a new color and new brush and paint the next space between the brown lines *(I)*. Continue painting up the entire leg, gently pivoting the leg from front to back as you paint, and using a different brush for each color. Transfer the insert to the other leg and continue painting. Allow the leggings to dry completely, 8 to 10 hours. Again, you can speed up drying with a fan or hair dryer.

7. FINISH: When the paint is dry, place the leggings in the dryer on high heat for 30 minutes to set the ink. Then, wash them alone with no other laundry (the ink may still bleed) on a gentle cycle with detergent, and then dry them again.

Note: If the leggings are brighter or more saturated than you had intended, hand wash them to get some of the pigment out before heat setting them in the dryer. Make sure to wring them out really well and put them in the dryer right away.

BATIK-DYED BEACH BLANKET

WITH CAITLIN MOCIUN

Batik is an ancient wax-resist dyeing technique. When wax is applied to fabric and then dyed, the waxed areas resist the dye, leaving behind soft, imperfect, undyed areas. Batik textiles have a long history around the world, and their signature crackled style can bring to mind beach sarongs and hippie tapestries. Caitlin and I wanted to use batik in a modern, graphic way, so we used geometric-shaped cookie cutters—squares, rectangles, circles, triangles, and hexagons—to stamp the fabric with wax (much faster than painting the wax on fabric by hand). Finding a pleasing combination of colors can take time, so we recommend that you test your design on scraps and make several samples before dyeing your beach blanket. (We like to test our patterns on 8" x 11"/20 cm x 27.5 cm fabric scraps and then use the printed scraps as napkins.)

MATERIALS:

Drop cloth

Dust mask

Rubber gloves

Apron

Hot plate (preferably with heat level options) or stovetop

2 yards (2 m) of 44" (112-cm)-wide flat-weave linen or cotton fabric, washed, dried, and ironed

Fabric scissors

Stainless steel geometric-shaped cookie cutters

Cookie sheet lined with aluminum foil

Heatproof bowl with a flat bottom, at least 6" (15 cm) wide

Batik wax

Cotton work gloves (optional)

4 foil roasting pans, approximately 13" x 17" (32.5 cm x 42.5 cm)*

Plastic or metal tub, approximately 15-gallon (60-L) size

1-quart (1-L) container and lid (clean, empty yogurt containers work well)

Paper plate (optional)

4 to 6 (^{2}⁄$_3$-ounce / 19-g) jars of Procion MX dye in colors of your choice

Soda ash

Noniodized salt

Large wooden or metal spoon*

Newsprint or scrap paper

Iron

Large pot*

Liquid castile soap

Candy or meat thermometer*

Hand-sewing needle or sewing machine

Thread in a color matching your finished fabric color

*Not to be used again for food

A) Cookie cutters on foil-lined cookie sheet

B) Dip cookie cutter in wax

C) Catch drops with lid

1. SET UP AND SAFETY: You will need a work surface of approximately 6' x 5' (1.8 m x 1.5 m), either on a table or on the floor. Lay down a drop cloth to protect your work surface. Batik wax can give off fumes when heated, so work in a well-ventilated room. Dyes and soda ash are harmful if they are inhaled, and soda ash can irritate the skin, so you might want to wear a dust mask and rubber gloves when mixing them. Cover anything nearby that you wouldn't want to have accidentally splashed with dye, and wear an apron to protect your clothes. Using a hot plate instead of the stovetop allows you to keep the hot wax right next to the fabric, but you could set up a worktable close to your stove instead. Keep the hot plate away from any table edges and always be careful not to burn yourself on the hot wax.

2. CUT FABRIC: Cut the fabric to 37" x 55" (94 cm x 140 cm) in order to make a 3' x 4½' (1 m x 1.4 m) blanket, leaving ½" (12 mm) on all sides as a seam allowance. Set aside your towel fabric. From the remaining fabric, cut several pieces of test fabric, approximately 8" x 11" (20 cm x 27.5 cm).

3. STAMP WAX ON TEST FABRIC: Place the cookie cutters on the cookie sheet *(A)*. Place the heat-proof bowl on the hot plate over medium heat. Place the wax in the bowl and allow it to melt (this will take about 10 minutes). When the wax has melted completely, turn the heat to the lowest possible setting (but do not allow the wax to harden).

Lay your test fabric on the drop cloth and smooth out any wrinkles. Place a cookie cutter in the wax and leave it there for several seconds *(B)*, allowing the cookie cutter to warm up (this will keep the wax from hardening as you transfer it to the fabric). You may want to use cotton gloves if the cookie cutters become too hot to touch. Lift the cookie cutter from the wax, holding a lid (or paper plate) under the cookie cutter as you move it from the bowl to the fabric to catch drips *(C)*. Place the cookie cutter on the test fabric, and press firmly until the wax is transferred to the fabric *(D)*. Leave the cookie cutters on the cookie sheet between uses. Experiment with how much pressure you use when you press down on the cookie cutter and how hot the wax is when it touches the fabric. Allowing the wax to dry slightly on the cookie cutter before pressing it onto the fabric can make the wax shapes sharper. If the wax dries white and appears to be sitting on the surface of the fabric *(E)* instead of being absorbed *(F)*, the wax is not hot enough. Practice stamping the fabric using all of the cookie cutter shapes until you are getting consistent and even wax stamps on your test fabric.

D) Stamp wax on fabric

E) Wax should not dry white on fabric's surface

F) Wax should be absorbed into the fabric

4. DYE TEST FABRIC: The wax-stamped fabric will be dyed, then stamped again, then over-dyed, so you will want to use lighter dye colors for the first round of dyeing and darker colors for the second. Keep in mind that the unwaxed finished fabric will be the color of the two dye baths combined *(Fig. 1)*. Mixing colors can be complex, so you may want to choose one control color (shown as blue in the illustration below) to simplify the process.

Set up small dye baths in the foil roasting pans, one for each color to be used in the first round of dyeing. Using the 1-quart (1-L) container, fill the roasting pans with enough water to submerge your test fabric, keeping track of how many quarts (liters) of water you add (4 quarts or liters equal 1 gallon). Follow the directions on the dye package to mix the dye, soda ash, and salt *(G)*. Saturate the stamped test pieces with fresh, cold water, and then place one in each dye bath *(H)*. Stir often with the large spoon and let the fabric sit in the dye for 1 hour (or as directed on package) *(I)*. Rinse the fabric in cold water until the water runs clear. Wring out excess water, then hang or lay the fabric flat to dry.

5. STAMP A SECOND LAYER OF WAX AND OVER-DYE TEST FABRIC: To add another color, repeat steps 3 and 4 after the test fabric pieces are completely dry. The areas where you applied wax initially will stay undyed (the color of the natural fabric); the areas where you applied wax the second time will be the color of the first dye bath; and the final background color will be a blend of the first and second dye baths.

Fig. 1: Examples of over-dyed colors, using blue as a control color

1st dye bath	2nd dye bath	final color		1st dye bath	2nd dye bath	final color
● +	● =	●		● +	● =	●

1st dye bath	2nd dye bath	final color		1st dye bath	2nd dye bath	final color
● +	● =	●		● +	● =	●

G) Mix dye *H) Submerge test fabric in dye* *I) First round of dyeing*

6. REMOVE WAX FROM TEST FABRIC: After the test fabric has been dyed and dried twice, place the test fabric pieces, one at a time, between two sheets of newsprint or scrap paper, and place the fabric and paper on an ironing board. Turn the iron to high and iron on top of the newsprint; do not iron directly on the wax, as this will damage the iron. The wax will melt and transfer from the fabric to the newsprint. Repeat with fresh pieces of newsprint or paper until all of the wax has been removed from the fabric. Repeat with all of the test pieces.

7. BATIK BLANKET: Choose the color combination and pattern that was most successful from your test pieces and repeat steps 3 to 6 using the blanket fabric. To remove the wax from the larger piece of blanket fabric, fill a large pot with water and add 1 teaspoon of liquid castile soap. Place the pot over medium-high heat, then place the fabric in the water. Bring the water temperature to 140°F (60°C), stirring the fabric occasionally. Check the fabric every few minutes to see if the wax has melted off. When the wax is removed, pour out the water and rinse the fabric in lukewarm water. Machine-wash and dry the blanket on its own (without other items) for just the first wash.

8. FINISH BLANKET: Fold each edge of the blanket a scant ¼" (6 mm) and a generous ¼" (6 mm) and iron the fold. Sew each edge with a straight stitch in a matching thread color.

CROCHETED OR BRAIDED RUGS

WITH CAL PATCH

For this project, Cal and I decided to show two great rug-making methods—braided and crocheted. Both methods use the same fabric but produce distinctively different looks. Braided rugs (like the one shown on the top at left) have a classic, old-fashioned appearance, while crocheted rugs (as shown on the bottom at left) look more modern. An advantage to crocheting is that the rug is formed as a connected spiral, so there's nothing to sew up at the end (as is the case with the braided rug). On the other hand, braiding is a simple motion that nearly everyone knows how to do, and crochet takes a bit more practice. Both styles can be made in large sizes for floor rugs, or smaller sizes for potholders, seat cushions, or bath mats.

Any fabric can be used for crocheted and braided rugs, but knit jersey is particularly satisfying to work with because of the way it rolls into a yarnlike tube when cut into strips. The jersey runs smoothly through your fingers as you work the strips together, and the rolled edges give the rugs a tidy appearance. All varieties of knit fabric work well for this project, including jersey and interlock in cotton, rayon, and wool. You can even use old T-shirts from a thrift store instead of buying new yardage, which saves money, and makes you feel good about giving them a second life. However, if you would prefer to work with longer strips, which require less stopping and starting as you work, you should buy new yardage.

MATERIALS:

CROCHETED RUG	BRAIDED RUG
Fabric scissors	Fabric scissors
3 to 6 yards (3 to 6 m) jersey fabric or 6–12 T-shirts, washed and dried	3 to 6 yards (3 to 6 m) jersey fabric or 6–12 T-shirts, washed and dried
Stitch marker	Masking tape
Size M/N/13 (9 mm) crochet hook	2 safety pins
	Needle
	Thread in a color matching or similar to the fabric

A) Cut fabric strips

B) Roll fabric into ball

C) Cut slits to join strips

1. CUT STRIPS: To make the rugs shown on page 67, you will need 90 to 150 yards (82.3 to 137.2 m) of fabric strips. If you are using fabric yardage, use the scissors to cut a strip approximately 1½" (4 cm) wide along the entire length of the fabric. Cut a second strip along the entire width of the fabric. Observe which strip curls into a more compact tube. Depending on the jersey you've chosen, the strips cut from both directions will curl nicely or one strip will curl more than the other. Continue cutting 1½" (4-cm)-wide strips along the direction that created the tightest curled tubes *(A)*. The width of the strips does not need to be exact—when the fabric curls, imperfections in your cutting will be nicely hidden. The cut fabric will resemble thick pieces of stretchy yarn.

If you are using old T-shirts, first cut off the hem, then begin cutting at a slight angle along the bottom edge of the T-shirt body and quickly widen the cut to a 1½" (4-cm)-wide strip. Cut in a spiral along the tube of the T-shirt body to create one continuous strip. Continue cutting T-shirts until you have 90 to 150 yards of fabric strips, cutting more as needed.

2. JOIN STRIPS: If your rug is going to be made entirely from the same fabric, you can join all of the strips in advance and roll the length of fabric into a ball *(B)*. If you plan to use multiple colors, either join them all in a random order from the start (and then watch and see what unfolds) or join new strips as you work to have more control over the colors.

To join a new strip of fabric, snip a ¼" to ½" (6 mm to 12 mm) slit in the end of a strip you want to join, about ½" (12 mm) from the end. Do the same with the strip you wish to join it to *(C)*. Now overlap the ends so that the two holes line up. Grab the opposite end of the bottom strip, push it down through both holes at once *(D)*, and pull it all the way through until it flips at the end and becomes a smooth, knotless join *(E)*.

CROCHETED RUG
Note: For crochet basics, see page 173.

Chain 2.

ROUND 1: Work 6 single crochets (sc) into the second chain from the hook *(F)*. Place a stitch marker in the last stitch to mark the end of round. Do not join at the end of this or any future rounds. (6 sc)

D) Join strips

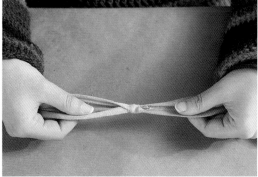

E) Pull to create a smooth join

F) Crochet, round 1

G) Crochet, round 2

H) Cal crocheting a rug

I) Continue to crochet outward

ROUND 2: In the first stitch of Round 1, work 2 single crochets, without joining or making a turning chain. Continue around, working 2 single crochets in every stitch *(G)*. Place a stitch marker at the end of the round. (12 sc)

ROUND 3: *Work 2 single crochets into the first stitch and 1 single crochet into the second stitch; repeat from * to end of round. Place a stitch marker at the end of the round. (18 sc)

ROUND 4: *Work 2 single crochets into the first stitch and 1 single crochet into each of the next 2 stitches; repeat from * to end of round. Place a stitch marker at the end of the round. (24 sc)

ROUND 5: *Work 2 single crochets into the first stitch, 1 single crochet into each of the next 3 stitches; repeat from * to end of round. Place a stitch marker at the end of the round. (30 sc)

Continue in this manner *(H + I)*, adding one more stitch between each increase for every round, until the rug is the desired size. When finished, taper the end by making 3 to 4 slip stitches, then cut the strip, leaving a 6" (15 cm) tail. Pull the tail through the last stitch and weave it in and out of the previous row using your fingers. The rug can be handwashed or washed by machine on the delicate cycle.

J) Braid strips *K) Secure ends with tape and safety pins* *L) Sew coiled strip*

BRAIDED RUG

1. START BRAID: Choose 3 strips of fabric and tape one end of the strips to a table. Fold the outside right strip over the center strip. Fold the outside left strip over the new center strip. Repeat, alternating right and left *(J)*. When you want to take a break, use a safety pin to secure the end of the strips together so the braid will not come undone *(K)*.

2. SEW BRAIDS INTO SPIRAL: When you have 5' (1.5 m) or more of braided fabric, it may become difficult to continue braiding depending on the size of your workspace. Use a safety pin to secure the beginning end of the strips together so the braid will not come undone. Remove the tape at the beginning of the braid and coil the braid end around itself, tucking the safety-pinned end underneath the center of the coil. Coil the entire length of the braid; it should lie loosely on your work surface. Thread a needle, doubling the thread for strength, and knot the end. Starting at the center, stitch down through one braid and up through the adjacent braid to connect them *(L)*. Pull the thread snug, but not too tight. Continue making large stitches approximately every ½" (12 mm) all the way along the coil. As you sew, check that the coil is lying flat—if it starts to bulge in the center, you are connecting the coil too tightly.

3. CONTINUE BRAIDING: When you finish sewing, tape the tail to your table. Continue braiding, adding new strips as you did before. When you finish another 5' (1.5 m) or so, stop and sew the braid into the coil. Make sure to continue sewing on the same side of the coil as you did in Step 2—the side of the rug with the stitches will be the underside of the rug.

4. FINISH RUG: When you are happy with the size of your braided rug, attach a safety pin to the end of the strips and trim the strips 1" (2.5 cm) past the safety pin. Sew the remaining braid to the coil. When you reach the end of the braid, tuck it over the edge toward the underside of the rug in a gradual curve. Sew the ends flat against the outermost braid. Turn the rug over so the stitches are on the bottom. The rug can be handwashed or machine-washed on the delicate cycle.

EMBROIDERY SAMPLER

WITH CAL PATCH

Cal taught more classes in my studio than any other teacher. We had lots of fun brainstorming ideas for classes, which was easy since Cal is experienced in nearly every fiber technique. The most popular class she taught, however, was the beginner embroidery class.

There's a lot to love about embroidery. It's inexpensive, portable, requires minimal supplies, and it takes just a short time to learn a dozen stitches (which is really all you need to know for a lifetime of embroidery). Samplers have been made for hundreds of years as a way to practice, record, and collect new embroidery stitches, and they're also a great project to do with others—you can talk as you stitch and then admire the end results together. Though embroidery is traditionally worked using a hoop to hold the fabric taut, Cal prefers to stitch without a hoop—the looser fabric makes it easier to simply dip the needle below the fabric's surface and immediately push it back up to the front, which makes the work go more quickly. A tip Cal gives new students is to embrace imperfection, celebrating the quirkiness and personality in handwork. She also suggests that you avoid working with thread longer than an arm's length—beginners often think they can avoid having to re-thread the needle by using a very long strand, but this leads to tangling and too much wear and tear on the thread.

MATERIALS:

Embroidery floss, in colors of your choice

Embroidery needle

¼ yard (¼ m) linen, or other fabric with a visible grain

Fabric scissors

Water-soluble (disappearing-ink) fabric pen (optional)

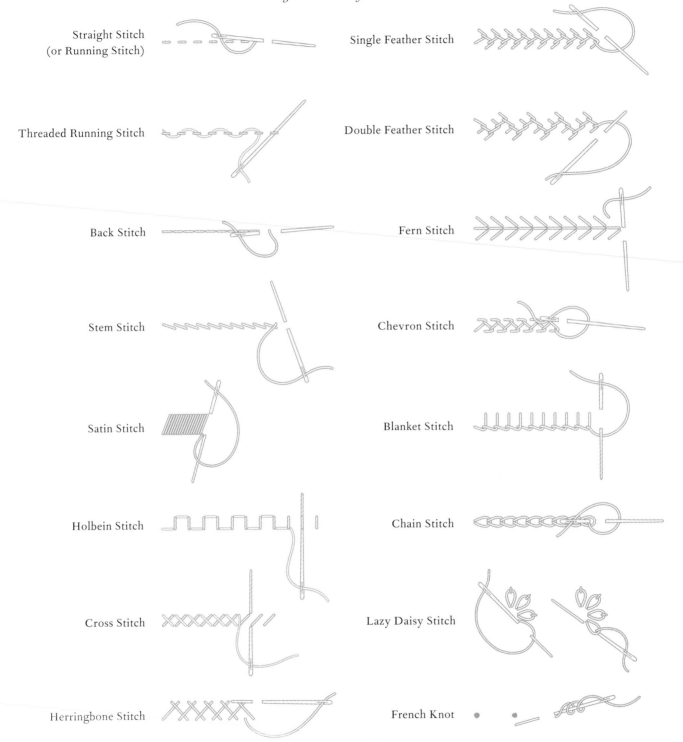

Fig. 1: Embroidery stitches

Straight Stitch (or Running Stitch)

Threaded Running Stitch

Back Stitch

Stem Stitch

Satin Stitch

Holbein Stitch

Cross Stitch

Herringbone Stitch

Single Feather Stitch

Double Feather Stitch

Fern Stitch

Chevron Stitch

Blanket Stitch

Chain Stitch

Lazy Daisy Stitch

French Knot

1. CUT FABRIC AND FLOSS: Cut a piece of fabric approximately 14" x 18" (35 cm x 45 cm) to use for your sampler. Cut a piece of floss approximately an arm's length (or 1 yard/1 meter) long. Thread the needle and knot one end of the floss. As you work, make sure that you are not accidentally including the thread tail with your stitches.

Note: If you would like to make stitches that are more delicate in appearance, you can adjust the thickness of the embroidery floss by removing one or more strands from the cut floss before threading the needle.

2. CREATE SAMPLER: A sampler is, by nature, a collection of stitches, so there is no need to practice on scrap fabric first. Before you get started, look at the stitches illustrated in *Fig. 1* and sketch out a design for your sampler using a water-soluble pen directly on the fabric. (Or you can "wing it" and create your design as you go!) As you work, think about ways that you can combine stitches to create a motif or a design (for examples, see *Fig. 2* below).

All of the stitches shown are worked from left to right, and begin by pushing the threaded needle from the back side of the fabric to the front. Pull the thread all the way through until the knot sits against the back side of the fabric. Traditionally, embroidery stitches are about ¼" (6 mm) long, though you can make your stitches longer or shorter if desired. The most important thing is to keep your stitch length consistent. When you finish a row of stitches or wish to change colors, pull the needle to the back side of the fabric and tie a firm knot as close to the fabric as possible. Weave the thread tail under nearby stitches and trim the ends.

3. FINISH: Check that all of your knots on the back side of the fabric are tight, and trim any excess floss. Your finished sampler can be framed and hung up, or you can use it as the front of a pillow or as part of a quilt.

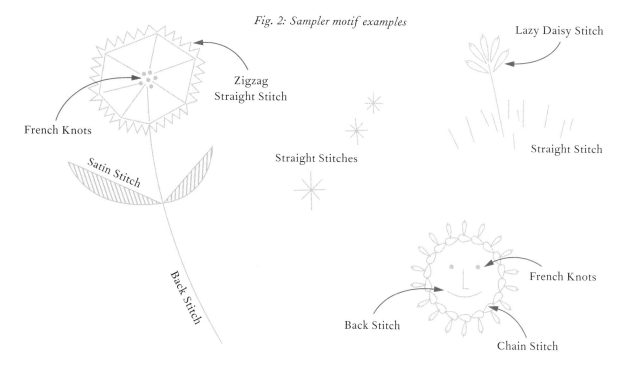

Fig. 2: Sampler motif examples

Lazy Daisy Stitch

Zigzag
Straight Stitch

French Knots

Straight Stitch

Satin Stitch

Straight Stitches

Back Stitch

French Knots

Back Stitch

Chain Stitch

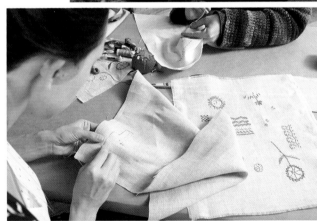

Embroidery can be a quiet and absorbing craft, but it's also very enjoyable to do in a group. In Cal's classes, students focus intently on their work while chatting away and occasionally comparing stitches.

FABRIC ORIGAMI

WITH WENDY HANSON

One of Wendy's first experiments with fabric origami came while she was sewing a wedding dress for her future sister-in-law. The dress featured flowers she had cut from Japanese obi fabric and sewed around the hem. On the wedding day, Wendy surprised the bride with fabric origami butterflies she had made from the obi scraps. Since then, Wendy has continued experimenting with three-dimensional fabric creations, making stunning art pieces in the form of birds, bees, and a large hive. For this project, she folded fabric into butterflies, then grouped them together into a mobile using driftwood and gold thread. Woven fabrics with a little stiffness work best for origami—we recommend medium-weight upholstery fabric, cotton broadcloth, linen, silk organza, or silk shantung. Slippery fabrics, such as silk chiffon or silk charmeuse, won't hold shape as well.

MATERIALS:

BUTTERFLIES

1 yard (1 m) muslin or ironing board

Iron

Ruler

Pencil

8½" x 11" (or A4) piece of card stock

Paper scissors

Spray starch

¼ yard (¼ m) woven fabric, such as medium-weight upholstery fabric, cotton broadcloth, linen, silk organza, or silk shantung

Fabric scissors

Sewing needle

Thread in a color matching the fabric

MOBILE

Driftwood piece, approximately 6" x 1¼" (15 cm x 3 cm)

Awl, or small Phillips-head screwdriver

10" (25 cm) of 2 mm natural hemp twine

20" (50 cm) of 1 mm gold twine

Embroidery needle

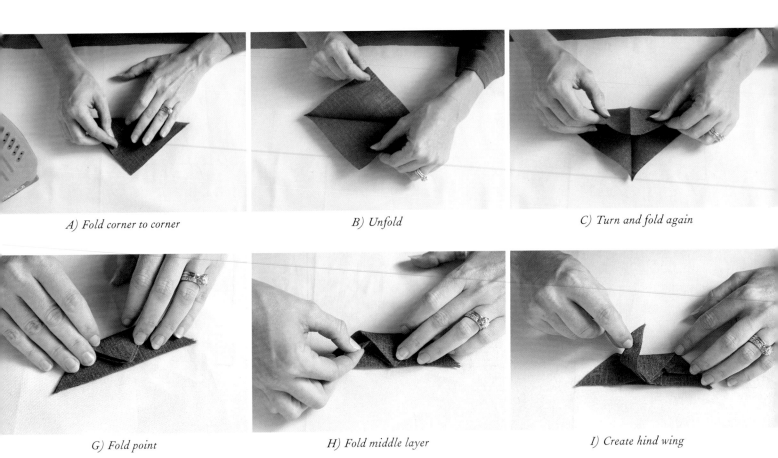

A) Fold corner to corner   *B) Unfold*   *C) Turn and fold again*

G) Fold point   *H) Fold middle layer*   *I) Create hind wing*

1. SET UP: You will need a work surface approximately 2' (60 cm) square for this project. Fold the muslin in half and lay it on the table to create a fabric-covered surface on which to iron, or use an ironing board if you prefer. Heat your iron so it is hot and ready when needed.

2. CREATE A PATTERN: Using the ruler, draw a perfect 5" (12.5 cm) square on the piece of card stock. (Using a corner of the paper will help ensure that the square has true 90-degree corners.) Carefully cut out the square with paper scissors. *Note: A 5" (12.5 cm) square will yield a butterfly with a 4½" (11 cm) wingspan; to make larger or smaller butterflies, adjust the size of the square, and be sure to use heavier fabric for larger butterflies.*

3. CUT FABRIC: Spray a light coating of spray starch onto the woven fabric. Iron the fabric until the starch is dry and there are no creases. Lay the square pattern on the fabric so the sides of the square are parallel to the grain of the fabric. Lightly trace around the edge of the pattern with a pencil and cut out the square with fabric scissors. Spray the fabric square with spray starch and iron again. (For some fabrics it may be helpful to spray and iron both sides, so it takes on an almost paperlike quality.)

D) Unfold   *E) Tuck sides to form triangle*   *F) Press*

J) Create other hind wing   *K) Pinch center*   *L) Stitch to secure folds*

4. FOLD BUTTERFLY: Fold the fabric square in half, corner to corner *(A)*. Iron the crease. Unfold *(B)* and rotate the square 90 degrees. Fold the square in half again, corner to corner, adding another crease perpendicular to the first crease *(C)*. Iron the second crease, being careful not to iron out the first crease you created. Unfold *(D)*.

Fold the square in half horizontally. Put both thumbs under the sides of the rectangle and bring them toward each other, forming a triangle *(E)*. With the point facing toward your body, press the triangle flat with the iron, heavily creasing the folded edges *(F)*. Turn over and press the back side if necessary.

Fold the triangle point to meet the center of the long, horizontal edge *(G)*. Press the new fold with the iron.

Grab the middle layer of fabric on one side of the triangle and fold it over, so the edge of the middle layer is parallel with the raw edge of the triangle *(H)*. Press the new fold with the iron. Repeat on the other side of the triangle.

Grab the top layer of one of the folds you just made and fold it along the vertical center line, creating the hind wings of the butterfly *(I)*. Press the new fold with the iron. Repeat on the other side *(J)*. Press both front and back. Your origami should now resemble a butterfly.

Pick up the butterfly and fold the wings backward to meet each other by folding the butterfly in half. Iron the fold. Pinch the butterfly at the thick center with one hand (this will be the body of the butterfly) and press the wings back out with your other hand *(K)*. Next, fold the wings toward the front to create a new acute angle fold. Iron the crease on both sides. This is the thickest fold, with the most layers of fabric, so use steam from the iron to help flatten it.

5. SEW BUTTERFLY: Thread your sewing needle with a length of thread, double it for extra strength, and knot the end. At the top third of the butterfly body, make a few stitches to secure the folds *(L)*. These stitches will be hidden if you make them along the crease you just created. Trim any frayed edges with scissors.

6. CREATE MOBILE: Follow Step 2 to create two additional butterfly templates, one 4½" (11 cm) square and the other 4" (10 cm) square. Follow Steps 3–5 to make the other two butterflies.

Carefully create a hole in the center of the driftwood using an awl or a Phillips-head screwdriver. Hold the awl upright and twist the tip back and forth until it reaches the other side. Fold the twine in half and push the folded end through the hole in the driftwood, creating a 3" (7.5 cm) loop. Tie a tight knot on the underside of the wood, and trim the excess twine.

Thread the embroidery needle with the gold thread (do not double the thread) and knot the end. Make two ⅛" (3-mm)-long stitches in the crease between the wings on the smallest butterfly, first near the center of the wings and then at the top. Repeat with the two larger butterflies, spacing them approximately 3" (7.5 cm) apart on the gold thread. When all three butterflies are attached to the gold thread, push the needle into the hemp twine knot at the base of the driftwood, and stitch through the knot several times to secure it *(Fig. 1)*. Trim the excess gold thread at both ends.

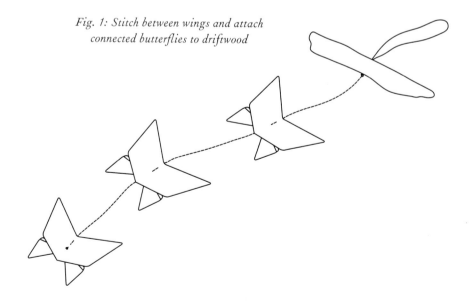

Fig. 1: Stitch between wings and attach connected butterflies to driftwood

SEWN CHILDREN'S
TOPS AND BOTTOMS

WITH WENDY HANSON

Wendy taught a popular class in my studio that we called Sewing Perfect Basics, in which students followed patterns designed by Wendy to make classic, simple, and polished garments. This project is based on the same concept, but instead we're making tops and bottoms for babies and toddlers. Because you don't need much fabric when you're making children's clothing, you can choose a really special fabric that might be too expensive for an adult garment. Wendy suggests using soft, lightweight fabrics made from natural fibers (cotton lawns, lightweight poplins, gauzes, and fine-gauge knits are great). The elastic openings on these garments are very functional for pulling on and off a squirmy child, and French seams give the garments a high-end look, both inside and out. The instructions include two types of bottoms (pants and bloomers) and two styles of tops (a tank and a dress), in sizes 6–12 months and 12–18 months.

MATERIALS:

Pattern paper

Pencil

Ruler

Paper scissors

Tape

Fabric scissors

Straight pins

Sewing machine

Matching thread

Iron

Small safety pins

PANTS/BLOOMERS

¾ yard (¾ m) 45" (112-cm)-wide fabric, washed, dried, and ironed (for Pants)

½ yard (½ m) 45" (112-cm)-wide fabric, washed, dried, and ironed (for Bloomers)

¼" (6-mm)-wide soft-stretch elastic, approximately 21" (52.5 cm)

½" (12-mm)-wide soft-stretch elastic, approximately 17" (42.5 cm)

TOP/DRESS

½ yard (½ m) 45" (112-cm)-wide fabric, washed, dried, and ironed (for Top)

¾ yard (¾ m) 45" (112-cm)-wide fabric, washed, dried, and ironed (for Dress)

⅛" (3-mm)-wide soft-stretch elastic, approximately 11" (27.5 cm)

A) Pin pattern piece to fabric

B) Wendy prepares pattern pieces

C) Sew side seams

PANTS AND BLOOMERS

1. CREATE PATTERN(S): Lay the pattern paper over the patterns on page 165 and use a pencil and ruler to trace the pattern pieces for the garment(s) you would like to make, choosing the appropriate size and style. Be sure to transfer all the information on the pattern sheet, including the elastic lengths. Once you have transferred the pattern, cut out the pattern pieces using your paper scissors and tape the pieces together if necessary.

2. CUT FABRIC AND ELASTIC PIECES: Fold the fabric in half, with right sides together and selvedges aligned, and place the edge of the pattern piece marked "fold" along the folded edge of the fabric. Pin the pattern piece to the fabric with straight pins *(A + B)*, and use fabric scissors to cut around the edge of the pattern. Cut out a second piece in the same way for the back.

Stretch the elastic pieces a few times, then cut them to the lengths indicated on the pattern sheet.

3. SEW GARMENT: Lay the two fabric pieces you just cut on top of each other with wrong sides facing and the edges aligned. Pin the side seams together with straight pins. Using a straight stitch, sew the side seams ⅛" (3 mm) from the edge *(C)*, removing the straight pins as you go (it will look like you've sewn your garment with the seams on the outside). Pin and sew the inseam the same way. After sewing the inseam, you will need to steam and stretch it a bit to keep the inseam curve from buckling. Press all the seam allowances flat to one side.

Turn the garment wrong side out and press the seams flat at their fold. Using a straight stitch, sew the side seams and inseams ¼" (6 mm) from the edge. You're now making what's called a French seam, which conceals the first seam's raw edges inside the second seam (see *Fig. 4* on page 33).

4. PRESS FABRIC: Fold and press the leg openings ¼" (6 mm) to the wrong side *(D)*, and then ⅜" (10 mm) to the wrong side, creating tunnels for the elastic. Fold and press the waist opening ¼" (6 mm) to the wrong side, and then ⅝" (16 mm) to the wrong side, creating a tunnel for the elastic. Pin the waist and leg opening folds in place *(E)*.

5. SEW WAIST AND LEG OPENINGS: Turn the bloomers/pants wrong side out and using a straight stitch, sew the waist ⅝" (16 mm) from the edge; leave a 1" (2.5 cm) opening for inserting the elastic. Add another row of stitching to the waist, 1/16" (1.5 mm) from the edge.

D) Fold and press leg openings

E) Pin folds

F) Remove machine base to sew leg openings

G) Thread elastic through tunnel

H) Sew elastic ends in place

I) Even out gathers

Take off the outer portion of the base of your machine in order to sew the tiny leg openings on the machine's free arm *(F)*. Sew the leg openings ⅜" (10 mm) from the bottom edge and then again 1/16" (1.5 mm) from the edge, leaving a 1" (2.5 cm) opening at each inseam for inserting the elastic.

6. ADD ELASTIC: Attach a safety pin to one end of the ½" (12-mm)-wide waistband elastic. Slowly thread the elastic through the tunnel with the safety pin *(G)*, being careful not to fold or twist the elastic. Secure the end of the elastic at the tunnel opening with a straight pin. Continue to thread the elastic through the tunnel, gathering the fabric on the elastic as you go. After the safety pin and leading end of the elastic are through the tunnel, pull a couple inches of elastic out of each end of the tunnel. Overlap the elastic ends ½" (12 mm) and secure them with a safety pin. Before you sew and cut your elastic, try the bloomers/pants on the child. You may need to adjust the elastic to make it snugger or looser. When the elastic fits as desired, hand-sew it in place *(H)*.

Repeat Step 6 to add ¼" (6-mm)-wide elastic to the leg openings.

Once your elastic pieces are secured, even out the gathers along the elastic *(I)*. Stretch out the elastic a bit and stitch the tunnel openings closed with a straight stitch.

A) Cut out pattern pieces

B) Fold and press armholes

C) Sew armholes

TOP AND DRESS

1. CREATE PATTERN(S): Lay the pattern paper over the patterns on page 162 and use a pencil and ruler to trace the pattern pieces for the garment(s) you would like to make, choosing the appropriate size and style. Be sure to transfer all the information on the pattern sheet, including the elastic length. Once you have transferred the pattern, cut out the pattern pieces using your paper scissors and tape the pieces together if necessary.

2. CUT FABRIC AND ELASTIC PIECES: Fold the fabric in half with wrong sides facing and the selvedges aligned, and place the edge of the front pattern piece marked "fold" along the folded edge of the fabric. Pin the pattern piece to the fabric with straight pins, and use fabric scissors to cut around the edge of the pattern *(A)*. Cut out a second piece in the same way using the back pattern piece.

Stretch the elastic piece a few times, then cut the elastic to the length indicated on the pattern sheet.

3. PRESS FABRIC: Press the armholes ⅛" (3 mm) to the wrong side, using steam to help smooth the fabric along the curve *(B)*. Slightly snip the raw edge of the fabric at the most acute part of the curve to help it lie flat, then fold the armhole another ³⁄₁₆" (4.5 mm) to the wrong side and press. Pin the armhole hem in place, if needed. Repeat for the other armhole.

Press the bottom hem ¼" (6 mm) to the wrong side, then fold again 1¼" (3 cm) to the wrong side.

Press the neckline ⅛" (3 mm) to the wrong side. Slightly snip the fabric's edge at the curve's most acute part to help it lie flat, then fold again ¼" (6 mm) to the wrong side, pinning if needed.

4. SEW GARMENT: Lay the two fabric pieces on top of each other with wrong sides facing. Pin the side seams together with straight pins. Using a straight stitch, sew the side seams ⅛" (3 mm) from the edge, removing the pins as you go. Repeat on the shoulder seams. (It will look like you've sewn your garment with the seams on the outside.) Press all of the seam allowances flat to one side.

Turn the garment wrong side out and press all of the seams flat at their fold. Using a straight stitch, sew the side seams and shoulder seams ¼" (6 mm) from the edge. You've now made what's

D) Sew hem

E) Thread elastic through neckband tunnel

F) Stitch opening closed

called a French seam, which neatly conceals the first seam's raw edges inside the second seam (see *Fig. 4* on page 33).

5. SEW ARMHOLES, HEM, AND NECKLINE: Take off the outer portion of the base of your machine and sew the tiny arm openings on the machine's free arm.

Using a straight stitch, sew along the edge of the armhole fold, ⅛" (3 mm) from the edge *(C)*. These are tricky curves, so go slow and be patient. Once you have finished sewing, press the armhole using steam. Repeat for the other armhole.

Using a straight stitch, sew the hem 1¼" (3 cm) from the edge *(D)*. If your machine does not have a guide for 1¼" (3 cm), you can create one by placing a piece of tape ¾" (2 cm) from the presser foot and drawing a line on the tape parallel to the presser foot, 1¼" (3 cm) away from the sewing needle. Be sure to use a permanent marker so the ink does not rub off on your garment.

Using a straight stitch, sew the neckline ¼" (6 mm) from the folded edge. At one shoulder seam, leave a ½" (12 mm) opening for inserting the elastic. Press your seam nicely before inserting the elastic.

6. ADD ELASTIC: Attach a small safety pin to one end of your neckband elastic. Slowly thread the elastic through the tunnel with the safety pin, being careful not to fold or twist the elastic *(E)*. As you work the length of the elastic through the tunnel, secure the end of the elastic at the tunnel opening with a straight pin. Continue to thread the elastic through the tunnel, gathering the excess fabric as you go. After the safety pin and leading end of the elastic are through the tunnel, pull an inch or so of the elastic out of each end of the tunnel. Overlap the elastic ends ½" (12 mm) and secure them with a safety pin. Before you sew and cut your elastic, try the garment on the child to make sure it fits, adjusting the elastic to make it snugger or looser, as needed. When the garment fits as desired, hand-sew the elastic in place.

Once your elastic is secured, even out the gathers along the elastic. Stretch out the elastic a bit and stitch the tunnel opening closed with a straight stitch *(F)*.

BRASS AND SILK JEWELRY

WITH JENNIFER SARKILAHTI

Jennifer introduced me to Metalliferous, a mecca of jewelry components in New York City's Diamond District. The store is jam-packed with great materials but can be a bit overwhelming. To help beginners avoid feeling paralyzed by the options at Metalliferous—or any jewelry supply store—Jennifer suggests starting with two affordable, appealing, and easy-to-find materials: brass and silk. Silk thread can be easily found in a variety of colors and thicknesses, and it pairs beautifully with brass beads. The instructions here show you how to make bracelets and necklaces, but once you learn the technique, you'll likely start designing pieces of your own. Note that brass is sometimes blended with nickel, which can cause skin irritation, so if you know you have a sensitivity, Jennifer recommends using sterling silver and oxidizing the finish to make it darker.

MATERIALS:

Table lamp

1' (30.5 cm) square piece of felt

Small dishes or cups

Clear nail polish

Small scissors

Silk stringing thread, such as Griffin Silk Thread size No. 6, in a variety of colors

Crimping pliers

Needle-nose pliers

Heavy-duty scouring pad or plain steel wool (optional)

Jewelry polishing cloth (optional)

An egg, saucepan, and small plastic container for oxidizing silver (optional)

BEADS TO STRING ON SILK*

Large brass open hexagons 22 mm x 2 mm

Small brass open hexagons 13 mm x 2 mm

Brass pendants

Small brass hexagon beads with drilled center holes

Brass tube beads

Brass cube beads 4 mm x 4 mm

Diagonal cut brass tube beads

COMPONENTS TO FINISH ENDS*

Brass hook clasps

Closed jump rings

Brass crimp beads

*We recommend buying an assortment of these materials and experimenting to create a variety of finished pieces (see Resources on page 175).

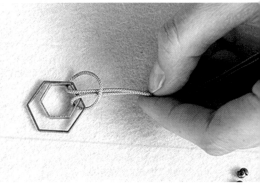

A) Jewelry-making setup   *B) Experiment with bead arrangements*   *C) Attach a bead with a slipknot*

1. SET UP: You will need a work surface of approximately 2' x 3' (60 cm x 90 cm). Working with small pieces can strain your eyes, so it's best to work under a table lamp. A padded surface, such as a piece of felt, helps prevent beads from rolling away, and small dishes or cups can be used to hold beads *(A)*.

2. CHANGE THE FINISH OF THE METAL: If the brass is too shiny, rub the surface of the brass shapes with a heavy-duty scouring pad or steel wool several times in the same direction until you achieve the desired finish.

If the brass is not shiny enough, rub the brass shapes with a polishing cloth until you achieve the desired finish. Note that, over time, you can restore the luster on the surface of your brass jewelry by rubbing it with a polishing cloth.

If you are using sterling silver instead of brass, it's possible to darken the finish. To do so, boil an egg for 10 minutes. Remove the egg from the pan and cut it into four pieces (cut through the shell, leaving the shell attached). Place the pieces of egg around the edges of a small airtight container. Place the silver jewelry pieces in the center of the container, not touching the egg. Close the lid and leave it for 30 to 40 minutes or until the desired patina is achieved. Remove the pieces from the container and polish them gently with a soft polishing cloth to even out the surface.

3. PREPARE THREAD AND MAKE BRACELETS AND NECKLACES: Soak the silk thread in water and run your fingers along the length of the strand to remove any wrinkles; hang it to dry. If using Griffin Silk Thread, cut off the attached needle.

When creating bracelets or necklaces, you need to determine the length of the silk thread required, which beads to string onto the thread, and how to finish the ends. (See the photo on page 86 for examples of these combinations.) For necklaces, we recommend a thread length between 22" (55 cm) to 28" (70 cm), plus 4" (10 cm) for finishing the ends. For bracelets, we recommend that you choose a thread length based on your wrist circumference; the sample on pages 86 and 91 is 7" (17.5 cm), plus 4" (10 cm) for finishing the ends.

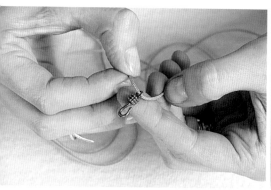

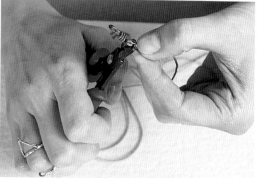

D) Slip clasp onto silk

E) Attach clasp with crimp bead

F) Jennifer pulls the ends of a pull-clasp closure

Place beads on your work surface and experiment with different arrangements of the beads *(B)*. When you find a grouping that you like, string them on to the silk thread. Beads with large holes and pendants (like the open hexagon beads and pyramid-shaped pendant on page 87) can be attached to the thread with a slipknot *(C)*.

4. FINISH ENDS: In this project, the ends of the silk thread are finished one of three ways: with a hook clasp, a knot, or a pull clasp.

TO MAKE A HOOK CLASP: A hook clasp is made using two end components: a hook and an eye. Hold the strung beads up to your neck or wrist to make sure you like the length (taking into consideration that the ends will be trimmed when the clasp is attached). Place a crimp bead over one end of the silk. Thread the silk through the loop of a clasp *(D)* and back through the crimp bead. Close the crimp bead with crimping pliers by first flattening the bead and then turning the pliers and folding the bead in half *(E)*. Turn the pliers again and fold the crimp bead in half one more time to create a secure end *(Fig. 1)*. Tie a double knot with the thread end beneath the bead and clip the thread end close to the knot. Secure the knot with a dot of clear nail polish.

Repeat with the other end of the silk, substituting a closed jump ring for the clasp.

Fig. 1: Closing a crimp bead

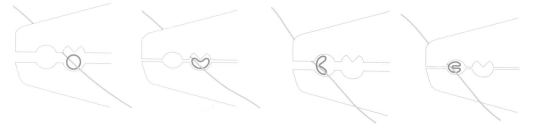

Fig. 2: Overhand knot

TO MAKE A KNOTTED END: Hold the strung beads up to your neck or wrist to make sure you like the length. Tie the silk ends in an overhand knot *(Fig. 2)* at the desired length and clip off any excess thread. Place a crimp bead over both ends of the silk. Close the crimp bead with crimping pliers by first flattening the bead and then turning the pliers and folding the bead in half. Turn the pliers again and fold the crimp bead in half one more time to create a secure end *(Fig. 1)*. Secure the knot with a dot of clear nail polish. Brush the ends of the thread with clear nail polish and allow them to dry. When dry, trim the ends to approximately ½" (12 mm) long, cutting through the dried nail polish.

TO MAKE A PULL-CLASP END: A pull clasp is made by inserting the thread ends through a bead and knotting off, which allows you to adjust the length of the bracelet or necklace *(F)*. Hold the strung beads up to your neck or wrist to make sure you like the length (taking into consideration that the ends will be trimmed when the pull clasp is attached). Thread one end of the silk through a 4 mm x 4 mm bead, then thread the other end of the silk through the same bead in the opposite direction. Tie a knot near the end of each silk thread, and secure the knots with a dot of clear nail polish. Brush the ends of the thread with clear nail polish and allow them to dry. When dry, trim the ends to approximately ½" (12 mm) long, cutting through the dried nail polish.

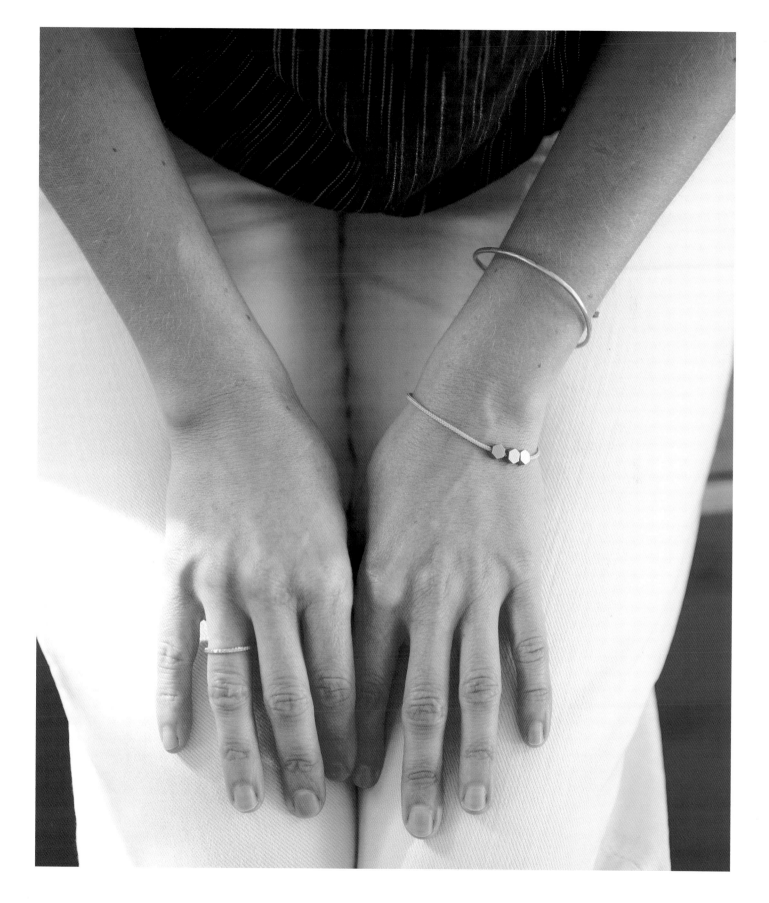

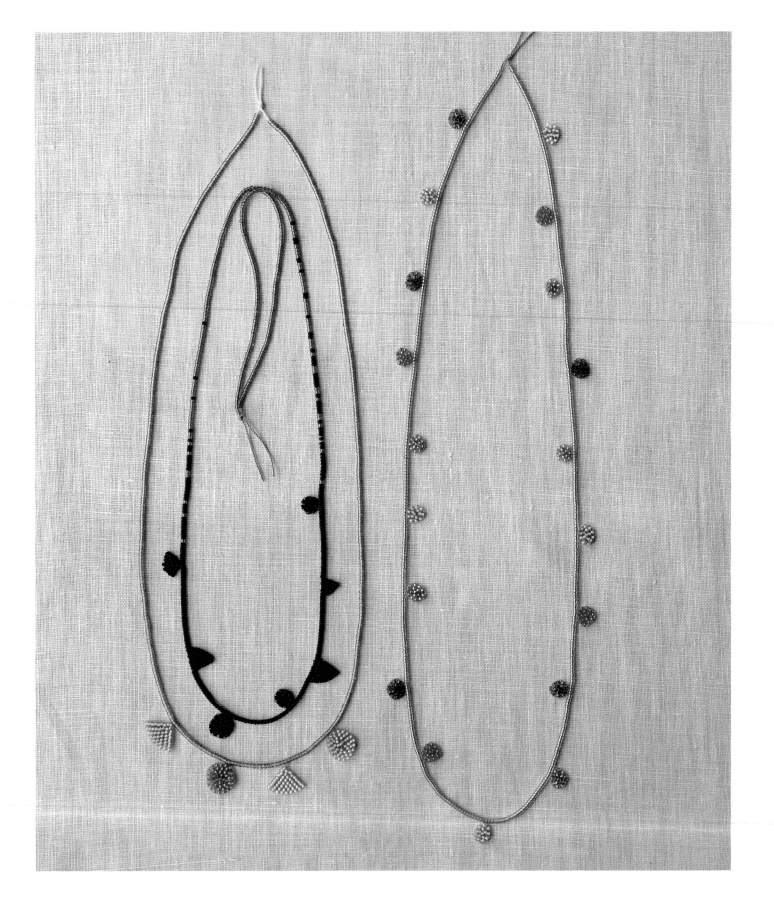

BRICK-STITCH BEADED NECKLACES

WITH JENNIFER SARKILAHTI

Jennifer is a master at many types of jewelry making, so deciding what to include in this book was a tough choice. Jennifer and I both have an appreciation for beaded jewelry—especially traditional Native American beading—but what ultimately led us to this project was a necklace that artist and shop-owner Chau Nguyen gave to Jennifer. We loved her use of two-dimensional brick-stitch beaded shapes strung on a beaded strand. (This method is called brick stitch because the rows of beads are staggered like stacked bricks.) Learning to make the beaded shapes using small beads can be difficult, so practice with larger beads when you are first learning. Once you get the hang of the process, switch to the smaller beads and begin to build your necklace. With some time and practice the process becomes methodical and relaxing—and even addictive!

Note: Working with small pieces can strain your eyes so it's best to work under a table lamp. A padded surface, such as a piece of felt, helps prevent beads from rolling away, and small dishes or cups can be used to hold beads. If you are having trouble with the beads slipping around, run a small amount of beeswax along the thread with your finger to condition the thread before beading.

MATERIALS:

Table lamp

1' (30 cm) square piece of felt

Small dishes or cups

8/0 or 7/0 size beads for practicing

11/0 glass seed beads in a variety of colors

Pack of beading needles in assorted sizes
(long, easy-thread needles work well)

Small scissors

3 spools nylon stringing thread,
in off-white, beige, and black

3 packages size No. 6 stringing thread
with attached needle, such as Griffin Silk
Thread, in beige

Beeswax (optional)

Masking tape

Clear nail polish

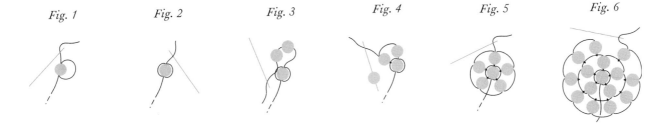

Fig. 1   Fig. 2   Fig. 3   Fig. 4   Fig. 5   Fig. 6

1. BEADING A BRICK-STITCH CIRCLE: Choose the nylon stringing thread color that best matches your bead choice. Cut a length of thread approximately 18" (45 cm) long. String one bead on your thread; pull it down the length of the thread, leaving a tail approximately 6" (15 cm) long.

CENTER BEAD: Pass the needle back up through the bead, creating an "ear" on one side of the bead *(Fig. 1)*. Bring the needle up through the bead again to create an ear on the other side *(Fig. 2)*.

FIRST ROUND: String 2 new beads onto the thread and pass the needle under one ear of thread on the center bead *(Fig. 3)*. Pull the needle through the thread and then back through the second new bead. Pull it taut. String a third new bead into the same ear of thread and pull it taut *(Fig. 4)*. Thread a fourth new bead, and push the needle under the other ear (on the other side) of thread and pull taut. String a fifth new bead into the same ear of thread and pull taut *(Fig. 5)*. You now have 5 beads surrounding the center bead; these 5 beads create the first round. Pass the needle down through the first bead in the round and thread it all the way through the other side. Pull taut.

SECOND ROUND: String 2 new beads onto the thread. Pass the needle under the bridge of thread between the beads from the first round. Pull taut. String a third bead and pass the needle under the next bridge from the first round. String a fourth bead and pass the needle under the same bridge. Continue adding 2 beads to each bridge from the first round, for a total of 9 to 11 beads in the second round *(Fig. 6)*. *Note: Although beads appear to be identical, they are all slightly different in size. As you approach the end of the second round, you may need one more or one less bead to make the circular shape.* Push the needle down through the top of the first bead of the second row, under the same bridge of thread, and then back up through the same bead.

THIRD ROUND AND FINISHING: Repeat the steps for the second round to make a third round, this time with 13 to 15 beads. On the last bead, push the needle down through the first bead in the round to the other side. To finish, remove the needle and leave the thread (which will later be used to attach the circle to the necklace). Thread the tail at the center of the circle onto the needle. Weave the needle in and out of the beaded circle until the thread feels secure and won't unravel. Trim the thread with scissors.

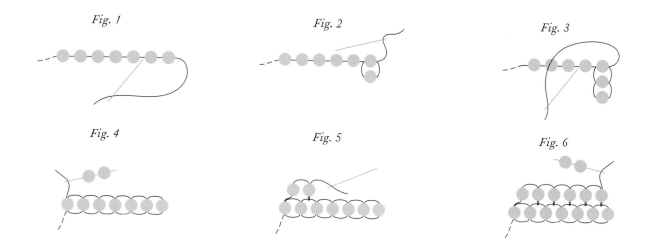

Fig. 1

Fig. 2

Fig. 3

Fig. 4

Fig. 5

Fig. 6

2. BEADING A BRICK-STITCH TRIANGLE: Choose the nylon stringing thread color that best matches your bead choice. Cut a length of thread approximately 18" (45 cm) long.

ANCHOR ROW: Use a "ladder stitch" to create the first row of beadwork. To do this, pick up 7 beads and position them approximately 6" (15 cm) from the end of the thread *(Fig. 1)*. Pass the needle up and down through the next bead and pull taut. The 7th bead will shift down next to the 6th bead *(Fig. 2)*. Continue passing the needle up and down through all the beads in the anchor row *(Fig. 3)*. You may need to adjust the positioning with your fingers to make a tight, neat row.

SECOND ROW: After creating the anchor row, pick up 2 new beads to start the second row *(Fig. 4)*. Pass the needle underneath the bridge of thread that runs between the second and third bead in the anchor row and pull the thread taut *(Fig. 5)*. Pass the thread back up through the second new bead. Pick up 1 new bead and pass the needle under the bridge of thread that runs between the next 2 beads and pull the thread taut. Repeat to the end of the row. You will now have an anchor row with 7 beads and a second row with 6 beads.

REMAINING ROWS: Continue beading the rows as in the second row, always picking up 2 beads for the first bridge and 1 bead for each bridge down the length of the row *(Fig. 6)*. Thread a single bead for the last, top row. Remove the needle and leave the tail (which will be used later to attach the beaded triangle to the necklace). Leave both tails from the thread so you have the option of attaching the beaded triangle to your necklace on either end.

Note: A triangle can easily be turned into a diamond shape. Follow the instructions above for making a triangle. When the triangle is complete, weave the thread back to the start of the anchor row, and build a second triangle off the reverse side of the anchor row to make a diamond.

3. STRING NECKLACE AND ATTACH BEADED SHAPES: Wet the size No. 6 stringing thread and smooth out any creases made from the packaging. Allow the thread to dry a bit (it does not need to be completely dry). Cut the thread approximately 36" (90 cm) from the needle end and discard the excess. Fold a small piece of masking tape over the thread, several inches from the end, to create a bead stop. Place beads on the stringing thread until you have reached your desired length. Place a piece of masking tape at the end and trim the thread 2" (5 cm) past the tape. Place the beaded strand on your work surface and plan a layout of your beaded shapes.

To attach a circle, thread the tail onto a beading needle and push the needle through the bead on the strand where you would like to attach the circle. Next, push the needle back into the same bead in the circle from which the tail came and pull it through. Weave the needle in and out of the beaded shape until it feels secure. Trim the thread with scissors. Lay the bead strand flat on your work surface and dab the connecting point with a drop of clear nail polish.

Triangles can be joined either at the tip of the triangle or along a side. To attach a triangle at the tip, follow the instructions above for attaching a circle. To attach a triangle along a side, you will need to weave in and out of the bead strand and the side of the triangle. Thread the tail onto a beading needle and push the needle through a bead on the strand where you would like to attach the triangle. Next, push the needle back into the second bead in the triangle shape and pull through. Weave the needle up and down the length of the triangle and the necklace strand. When you reach the end, weave the needle in and out of the beaded shape until it feels secure. Trim the thread with scissors. Lay the bead strand flat on your work surface and dab the connecting point with a drop of clear nail polish.

When all of the shapes are attached to the strand, remove the masking tape and tie the strand ends in a knot. Dab the knot with clear nail polish. Trim the ends to approximately ¾" (19 mm) and dab them with clear nail polish.

4. MAKE A NECKLACE WITH ALL SMALL CIRCLES: Make approximately 20 beaded circles, each with 2 rounds of beads and an outer round of 9 to 11 beads. Trim a stringing thread with attached needle to 36" (90 cm). Make a 29" (72.5 cm) strand of beads. Attach the circles to the necklace strand approximately 1½" (4 cm) apart.

5. MAKE A NECKLACE WITH TWO LARGE CIRCLES AND TWO LARGE TRIANGLES: Make 2 beaded circles, each with 4 rounds of beads and an outer round of 17 to 19 beads. Make 2 beaded triangles, each with an anchor row of 9 beads. Trim a stringing thread with attached needle to 36" (90 cm). Make a 27" (67.5 cm) strand of beads. Attach the circles and triangles to the middle of the necklace strand, approximately 1" (2.5 cm) apart.

6. MAKE A NECKLACE WITH TRIANGLES, CIRCLES, AND A DIAMOND: Make 2 beaded circles, each with 2 rounds of beads and an outer round of 9 to 11 beads. Make one beaded circle with 3 rounds of beads and an outer round of 13 to 15 beads. Make 3 triangles, one with an anchor row of 5 beads, one with an anchor row of 6 beads, and one with an anchor row of 7 beads. Make one beaded diamond with an anchor row of 5 beads. Trim a stringing thread with attached needle to 36" (90 cm) long. Make a 30" (75 cm) strand of beads. Attach the circles, triangles, and diamond to the necklace strand, spacing each one ½" to 1½" (12 mm to 4 cm) apart.

BEESWAX BIRTHDAY CANDLES

WITH JAIME RUGH

Jaime has great memories of making beeswax candles as a child, and over the years she has used beeswax for a variety of projects, from bookbinding to beading. For this project, she used beeswax to make small hand-dipped candles, which are perfect for placing atop a homemade birthday cake. Beeswax is naturally produced in the hives of honeybees, and it is sold in most art and craft supply stores. It smells wonderful while it melts and is completely nontoxic (unlike paraffin candle wax). Beeswax can vary in color from nearly white to brownish, but it is most often a shade of golden yellow, depending on the purity of the wax and the types of flowers pollinated by the bees. It can be fun to tint the candles by adding colored crayon shavings to the melting wax, especially when working with children.

MATERIALS:

Newsprint or wax paper

Hot plate (preferably with heat level options)
or stovetop

2 large cooking pots

1½ lbs (680 g) of 100% natural beeswax
(see Resources, page 175)

Clean, empty tin can, 28 ounces (840 ml)
or larger

Bamboo skewer

Scissors

20' (6 m) 100% cotton 15-ply wicking (flat
or square braiding; see Resources, page 175)

Pasta drying rack (optional)

A) Stir wax • *B) Dip in wax, then in ice water* • *C) Pull candles up along side of can*

1. SET UP: Cover your work surface with newsprint or wax paper. (Later, you can use hot water to clean any stray wax from your work surface.) If using a hot plate, keep it away from any table or counter edges and always be careful not to burn yourself on the hot wax.

2. MELT THE WAX: Fill one of the large pots with approximately 2" (5 cm) of water. Place the pot on the hot plate or stovetop over medium-high heat and bring the water to a slow boil. Place the beeswax in the tin can and set the can in the pot of boiling water. While the wax melts, fill the other large pot with ice water and set it near your workspace. Using a bamboo skewer, stir the wax occasionally until it has melted completely *(A)*, then turn the heat to low.

3. DIP THE CANDLES: Cut the wick into 9" (22.5 cm) pieces. Fold a piece of wick in half and hold it at the fold, so you have 2 conjoined 4½" (11 cm) wicks. Dip the wicks into the melted wax quickly 3 times and then place them in the ice water for a few seconds *(B)*.

Repeat the dipping and cooling process. The wax will begin to accumulate on the wick. Continue this way until the candles are approximately ¼" (6 mm) in diameter.

Note: To keep the candles straight and eliminate buildup at the base, try pulling the candles up along the side of the can as you dip them (C). If the wick begins to curl up or touch the other strand, you can dip the candles in ice water and gently separate them, or lay them flat on wax paper and softly roll them with your fingertips to straighten them out (the wax will still be slightly malleable). One more dip back into the hot wax should smooth out any unwanted imperfections. Always dip the candles in the cold bath before handling them so the wax doesn't burn your fingers.

4. FINISH CANDLES: Once the candles have reached the desired diameter, lay them on wax paper to harden; alternatively, hang them on a pasta drying rack. When the candles have hardened, snip the folded wick at the top of each pair with scissors. Save any leftover wax for future use by allowing it to harden in the can.

WOVEN PLACEMATS

WITH JAIME RUGH

Jaime first started weaving rugs on round peg looms as a young girl with her father. Though she did not expect to be drawn back to the basic over/under movements of weaving as an adult, she went on to study fiber arts in college, and weaving has become one of her primary interests. For this project, we created a loom by adding nails to two sides of an inexpensive silkscreen frame. Many rectangular looms have nails on all four sides, but Jaime prefers to place nails on only two sides of the frame, which allows her hands to move more freely back and forth. When looking for a frame, try to find one that has grooves along the middle of each side, which makes placing the nails easier. We used a lightweight cotton fabric for these placemats—should you have any leftover, the fabric ribbons are great for wrapping gifts. The finished placemats will be approximately 12" x 16" (30 cm x 40 cm).

MATERIALS:

12" x 18" (30 cm x 45 cm) silkscreen frame
(without the screen/fabric) or picture frame

1½" to 1¾" (4 cm to 4.5 cm) finishing nails
(zinc nails work well)

Hammer

Ruler (optional)

Pencil (optional)

¾ yard (¾ m) quilting-weight cotton fabric
per placemat, for the warp

1 yard (1 m) quilting-weight cotton fabric
per placemat, for the weft

Fabric scissors

Sewing machine

Iron

Spray starch (optional)

A) Hammer nails along
2 sides of frame

B) Cut fabric into strips

C) Sew warp strips together

1. MAKE LOOM: Place the silkscreen frame on your work surface. Hammer the first nail into the wood 1" (2.5 cm) from the corner on one of the long edges of the frame. Leave at least ¾" (19 mm) of the nail exposed. The nail should feel solid and secure, without poking through to the back side of the frame. Continue hammering nails every ½" to ¾" (12 mm to 19 mm) along the long edge of the frame until you are about 1" (2.5 cm) from the other corner. If you wish, use a pencil and ruler to mark the placement of your nails prior to using the hammer. Repeat along the other long edge of the frame *(A)*.

2. CUT FABRIC FOR WARP AND WEFT: In weaving terms, the warp is the set of lengthwise threads that holds the tension on a loom, while the weft is the thread that will be pulled through the warp to create the woven textile.

Lay out the patterned fabric and fold it lengthwise several times. Use fabric scissors to cut through the layers of fabric to create 1" (2.5-cm)-wide strips for the warp *(B)*. Imperfections won't be noticeable when the fabric is woven, so the strips do not need to be cut perfectly. Once all of the strips are cut, overlap 2 strip ends by 1" (2.5 cm) and use a sewing machine to sew a straight stitch back and forth several times at the overlap *(C)*. Cut and trim the thread and continue connecting the remaining pieces to form one long ribbon of fabric. Wrap the fabric ribbon into a ball.

Cut the solid-colored weft fabric into 1" (2.5-cm)-wide strips as you did for the warp fabric. Sew just 2 strips together to create a short ribbon; you will sew the rest of the strips together as you weave. (It may be helpful to have your loom set up next to your sewing machine as you weave.)

3. CREATE WARP: Arrange the loom with the nailed sides horizontally in front of you. Attach the patterned warp fabric to the first nail on the bottom left by tying a tight single knot; leave a few extra inches of fabric hanging. Pull the fabric up around the top nail on the left, then back down to the next nail on the bottom. Continue up and down from left to right *(D)*. When you reach the last nail, give the ribbon a good tug and tie a tight single knot *(E)*.

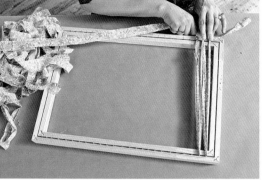

D) Create warp

E) Knot off warp

F) Weave weft

G) Make sure ribbon lays flat

H) Remove weaving from frame

I) Finish placemat

4. WEAVE WEFT: Starting on the bottom right, and working toward the left side of the loom, weave the 2 solid-color weft strips that you sewed together in Step 2 under and over the warp fabrics *(F)*. Continue to weave the fabric over and under until you reach the end of the row. Push the fabric down so it lays closer to the edge of the loom. At the end of the row, turn the weft ribbon and weave back in the opposite direction, alternating the over/under sequence. When you finish each row, use your hands to smooth the ribbon, making it lay fairly flat *(G)*. Do not pull the ribbon too tight or it will pull the sides of the weaving inward, and the finished shape won't be rectangular. When you start to run out of ribbon, bring the loom over to the sewing machine and sew another strip of weft fabric to the end of the previous ribbon.

5. FINISH PLACEMAT: The last row of weft might be difficult to weave because the space becomes tight. When the last row is complete, simply leave the extra weft ribbon hanging and pop your weaving up and off the frame *(H)*. Untie the corner knots and trim the edges so they are even. Fold the unfinished strips under and stitch them flat on the sewing machine *(I)*. Press both sides with an iron, using spray starch if you want the placemat to keep its form.

KNITTED CAT TOYS

WITH EMILY EIBEL + ILANA KOHN

I first met Emily and Ilana when they held a fabric marbling party at Ilana's apartment. I quickly learned that Emily was an experienced knitter and had recently made knitted cat toys as a gift for Ilana's cat, Wally. While coming up with the projects for this book, Emily knitted five adorable sample animals. It was very hard to choose which ones to feature in the book, but ultimately, we decided that our favorites were the bumblebee, hedgehog, and snail.

Making toys for pets is a fun way to try out knitting with double-pointed needles (see the knitting basics on page 169). The Bumblebee and Snail are great projects for beginners since they are small and only require knit and purl stitches. The Hedgehog features a slightly more advanced loop stitch, which is a fun way to add a spiked effect to the Hedgehog's back (your cat will also enjoy trying to pull out the loop stitches while playing). Fill the toys with catnip to make them even more enticing.

MATERIALS:

YARN

Madelinetosh Tosh Merino DK (100% superwash merino; 225 yards / 206 m; 100 grams): 1 hank each Charcoal (A), Silver Fox (B), and Butter (C)*

Koigu Premium Merino (KPM) (100% merino wool; 175 yards / 160 m; 50 grams): 1 hank #2400 (D)*

*Note: One hank of each color will be enough to make all three animals. Hedgehog uses A, B, and D; Bumblebee uses A, B, C, and D; Snail uses B and C.

NEEDLES

One set of five double-pointed needles size US 7 (4.5 mm)

NOTIONS

Stitch marker

Tapestry needle

Stuffing (cotton, wool, or kapok works best)

Catnip (optional)

A piece of crinkly acetate and a small bell (optional)

A) Four stitches on each needle   *B) Continue working loop pattern*   *C) Tie in new color*

HEDGEHOG

1. BODY: Using color A, cast on 6 stitches. Move the first 3 stitches onto a second needle. Your stitches are now divided between 2 needles.

Rotate your knitting so the tail is on the right side. Make sure that none of your stitches are twisted as you slip a third needle into the first stitch on the left side. Knit into this first stitch using the yarn attached to the needle on the right, pulling tightly to avoid gapping.

Your knitting is now joined in the round, and you will continue to work in rounds. When you reach the beginning of each needle, scoot your work to the tip of the needle closest to you and use your hands just as if you were knitting with only 2 needles (one with stitches in your left hand, and an empty needle in your right hand), ignoring the other needle. Knit the stitches onto the empty needle. When finished, push the stitches back to the middle of the needle and move on to the next one.

Place a marker on the first stitch to indicate the beginning of round (or simply use the hanging tail as your guide). Go on and knit to the end of the round.

SHAPE BODY

Note: A special technique called "Make Loop" (described below) is used to create the Hedgehog's spiny back. For less advanced knitters, this pattern can be simplified by replacing the loop stitches with knit stitches and then embroidering a simple repeating V pattern on his back.

MAKE LOOP: Insert the right-hand needle into the next stitch knitwise, bring the yarn between the needles to the front, around the tip of your left thumb, and to the back again between the needles, making a loop. (You can adjust the size of the loop at this point, before completing the stitch.) Hold the loop with your left thumb as you twist the right-hand needle forward to insert it into the front of the same stitch. Wrap the yarn around the needle as you would for a regular knit stitch, draw the yarn through the stitch and off your left-hand needle. You will have two stitches on your right needle, with a loop coming out from between them. Pick up the right stitch with your left-hand needle and pull it over the left stitch and off the needle. Gently tighten the stitch by tugging on the loop and your working yarn.

D) Start knitting with new color	*E) Emily shaping Hedgehog head*	*F) Stuff part way*

ROUND 1: Knit 1 front/back (knit into the front and back of the next stitch), Make Loop, knit 1 front/back, knit 1 front/back, Make Loop, knit 1 front/back—10 stitches (5 stitches on each needle).

ROUND 2: Knit 1, Make Loop, knit 1 front/back, knit 1, Make Loop, knit 1, Make Loop, knit 1 front/back, knit 1, Make Loop—12 stitches (6 stitches on each needle). Rearrange the stitches so that you have 4 stitches on each needle *(A)*.

CONTINUE HEDGEHOG LOOP PATTERN

ROUND 1: Make Loop, knit 1; repeat this pattern to the end of the round—18 stitches (6 stitches on each needle).

ROUND 2: Knit 1, knit 1 front/back; repeat this pattern to the end of the round.

ROUNDS 3 AND 4: Repeat Rounds 1 and 2—27 stitches (9 stitches on each needle).

ROUND 5: *Make Loop, knit 1; repeat from * 8 more times, knit 9.

ROUND 6: Knit all stitches.

ROUND 7: *Knit 1, Make Loop; repeat from * 8 more times, knit 9.

ROUND 8: Knit all stitches.

Repeat Rounds 5–8 for 1" to 1½" (2.5 cm to 4 cm), ending with Round 5 or 7 *(B)*. Cut a nice long tail, and tie in color B to the tail *(C)*.

2. SHAPE HEAD: Knit 3 rounds *(D + E)*.

ROUND 1: Knit 4, knit 2 together, knit 2, knit 2 together, knit 2, knit 2 together, knit 4, knit 2 together, knit 5, knit 2 together—22 stitches remain (8 stitches on first needle, 7 on second needle, and 7 on third needle).

ROUND 2: Knit all stitches.

ROUND 3: Knit 4, knit 2 together, knit 1, knit 2 together, knit 1, knit 2 together, knit 3, knit 2 together, knit 3, knit 2 together—17 stitches remain (7 stitches on first needle, 5 on second needle, and 5 on third needle).

ROUND 4: Knit all stitches.

ROUND 5: Knit 5, knit 2 together, knit 10—16 stitches remain (6 stitches on first needle and 5 each on second and third needles).

G) Add more stuffing *H) Pick up stitches for ears* *I) Pick up stitches for feet*

ROUND 6: Knit all stitches.

Stuff partly with stuffing *(F)*, a good portion of catnip (optional), and then top off with more stuffing *(G)*.

ROUND 7: Knit 1, knit 2 together, knit 1, knit 2 together, knit 1, knit 2 together, knit 2, knit 2 together, knit 1, knit 2 together—11 stitches remain (4 stitches each on first and second needles, and 3 on third needle).

ROUND 8: Knit 2, knit 2 together, knit 2 together, knit 2, knit 3—9 stitches remain (3 stitches each needle).

Add a bit more stuffing, along with catnip (optional), and a bell or small piece of acetate for a crinkly sound (optional).

ROUND 9: Knit 1, knit 2 together, knit 2 together, knit 4—7 stitches remain (2 stitches each on first and second needles, and 3 stitches on third needle).

ROUND 10: Knit 2 together, knit 2 together, knit 3—5 sts remain (1 stitch each on first and second needles, and 3 stitches on third needle). Cut a nice long tail. Using a tapestry needle, thread the tail through the remaining stitches and cinch the end of the nose closed. Pull tight to avoid a hole. Weave in the ends.

3. EARS: Pick up (but do not knit) 3 stitches on the left side of the Head. Tie color B yarn onto the stitch toward the center of the Head. Purl 3 *(H)*. Bind off all stitches knitwise, tying the yarn at the last stitch. Cut a nice long tail. Tie this tail to the first tail and using a tapestry needle, thread both tails down through the Head, trimming any excess.

Pick up (but do not knit) 3 stitches on the right side of the Head and repeat to create a second ear.

4. FEET: Decide on the placement of the Feet, then begin by picking up (but not knitting) 4 stitches horizontally across the area where you'd like the first Foot. Pick up 4 more stitches a row below the first 4 stitches *(I)*. Tie color B yarn onto the bottom right stitch *(J)*, join for working in the round, and place a marker on the first stitch. Knit 3 rounds. Cut a nice long tail. Using a tapestry needle, thread the tail through the 8 stitches and cinch the end of the Toe closed. Thread the tail through the Body, trimming any excess. Repeat this process for the remaining 3 Feet.

5. FEATURES: Using tapestry needle and color D, embroider a nose and eyes *(K + L)*.

J) Tie yarn onto stitch   *K) Embroider face*   *L) Finished eye*

BUMBLEBEE

1. BODY: Using color A, cast on 6 stitches. Move the first 3 stitches onto a second needle. Your stitches are now divided between 2 needles.

Rotate your knitting so the tail is on the right side. Make sure that none of your stitches are twisted as you slip a third needle into the first stitch on the left side. Knit into this first stitch using the yarn attached to the needle on the right, pulling tightly to avoid gapping.

Your knitting is now joined in the round, and you will continue to work in rounds. When you reach the beginning of each needle, scoot your work to the tip of the needle closest to you and use your hands just as if you were knitting with only 2 needles (one with stitches in your left hand, and an empty needle in your right hand), ignoring the other needle. Knit the stitches onto the empty needle. When finished, push the stitches back to the middle of the needle and move on to the next one.

Place a marker on the first stitch to indicate the beginning of round (or simply use the hanging tail as your guide). Go on and knit to the end of the round.

ROUND 1: Knit all stitches.
ROUND 2: Knit 1 front/back (knit into the front and back of the next stitch) across all stitches—12 stitches (4 stitches each needle).
ROUND 3: Knit 3, knit 1 front/back; repeat this pattern to the end of the round—15 stitches (5 stitches each needle).
ROUND 4: Knit all stitches. Cut a nice long tail. Tie in color C.
ROUNDS 5 AND 6: Knit all stitches. Cut a nice long tail. Tie in color A.
ROUNDS 7 AND 8: Knit all stitches. Cut a nice long tail. Tie in color C.
ROUNDS 9 AND 10: Knit all stitches. Cut a nice long tail. Tie in color A.
ROUNDS 11 AND 12: Knit all stitches.
ROUND 13: Knit 2 together, knit 3; repeat this pattern to the end of the round—12 stitches remain (4 stitches each needle).
ROUND 14: *Knit 2 together; repeat from * to end of round—6 stitches remain (2 stitches on each needle). Cut a nice long tail. Stuff the Body. Using a tapestry needle, thread the tail through the

remaining 6 stitches and cinch the end of the Body closed. Pull tight to avoid a hole. Thread the remaining tails through the Body, trimming any excess.

2. WINGS: Pick up (but do not knit) 5 stitches vertically along the back of the Body. Tie color B yarn to the last stitch.

ROW 1 (Right Side): Knit all stitches.
ROW 2: Slip 1 purlwise, purl to end of row.
ROW 3: Slip 1 knitwise, knit to end of row.
ROW 4: Slip 1 purlwise, purl to end of row.
ROW 5: Bind off 1 stitch, knit 1, knit 2 together—3 stitches remain. Bind off all stitches purlwise. Cut a nice long tail. Using a tapestry needle, thread the tail along the wrong side of the Wing, then through the Body, trimming any excess.

Beginning 2 rows away from the first Wing, work a second Wing as you did the first, making sure that the first Wing is closer to you when you work Row 1, with the purl side facing you, so that the knit sides of the Wings face each other.

If you wish, tie a strand of yarn between the Wings and attach a long strand of yarn or piece of elastic to the strand between the Wings, so that you can "fly" the Bumblebee around while your cat chases it.

SNAIL

1. BODY: Using color B, cast on 5 stitches. Move the first 3 stitches onto a second needle. Your stitches are now divided between 2 needles.

Rotate your knitting so the tail is on the right side. Make sure that none of your stitches are twisted as you slip a third needle into the first stitch on the left side. Knit into this first stitch using the yarn attached to the needle on the right, pulling tightly to avoid gapping.

Your knitting is now joined in the round, and you will continue to work in rounds. When you reach the beginning of each needle, scoot your work to the tip of the needle closest to you and use your hands just as if you were knitting with only 2 needles (one with stitches in your left hand, and an empty needle in your right hand), ignoring the other needle. Knit the stitches onto the empty needle. When finished, push the stitches back to the middle of the needle and move on to the next one.

Place a marker on the first stitch to indicate the beginning of round (or simply use the hanging tail as your guide). Go on and knit to the end of the round.

ROUND 1: Knit 1 front/back (knit into the front and back of the next stitch), knit 1, knit 1 front/back, knit 2—7 stitches.
ROUNDS 2–6: Knit all stitches.
ROUND 7: Knit 3, knit 1 front/back, knit 1, knit 1 front/back, knit 1—9 stitches.
ROUNDS 8–17: Knit all stitches.
Stuff the Body loosely with stuffing.
ROUND 18: Knit 2 together, knit 2 together, knit 2 together, knit 2 together, knit 1—5 stitches remain.

Cut a nice long tail. Using a tapestry needle, thread the tail through the remaining 5 stitches and cinch the end of the Body closed. Pull tight to avoid a hole. Thread the tail through the Body, trimming any excess.

2. SHELL: Using color C, cast on 5 stitches, leaving a nice long tail. Divide the stitches between 2 needles. Join for working in the round, place a marker on the first stitch, and begin knitting in the round.

ROUNDS 1–5: Knit all stitches.

ROUND 6: Knit 1, knit 1 front/back, knit 1, knit 1 front/back, knit 1—7 stitches.

ROUND 7–11: Knit all stitches.

ROUND 12: Knit 2, knit 1 front/back, knit 1, knit 1 front/back, knit 2—9 stitches.

ROUNDS 13–15: Knit all stitches.

ROUND 16: Knit 2, knit 1 front/back, knit 1, knit 1 front/back, knit 1, knit 1 front/back, knit 2—12 stitches.

ROUNDS 17–22: Knit all stitches.

ROUND 23: Knit 4, knit 1 front/back, knit 2, knit 1 front/back, knit 4—14 stitches.

ROUNDS 24–26: Knit all stitches.

ROUND 27: Knit 5, knit 1 front/back, knit 2, knit 1 front/back, knit 5—16 stitches.

ROUNDS 28–31: Knit all stitches.

Fill the body three-quarters full with stuffing, add catnip (optional), then top off with more stuffing.

ROUND 32: *Knit 1, knit 2 together; repeat from * 4 more times, knit 1—11 stitches remain.

ROUND 33: *Knit 2 together; repeat from * 4 more times, knit 1—6 stitches remain.

Cut a nice long tail. Using a tapestry needle, thread the tail through the remaining 6 stitches and cinch the end of the Shell closed. Pull tight to avoid a hole. Do not weave in the ends.

3. FINISHING: Thread the cast-on tail through a tapestry needle, roll the cast-on end into the middle of the Shell, and tack it down, securing it. Continue to create a spiral, sewing the two sides of the Shell together to anchor the spiral as you go. Thread the finishing tail through a tapestry needle and sew the end of the Shell to the spiral. Tie a knot to secure the spiral. Using color B, sew the Shell to the Body. Thread the tail through the Body, trimming any excess.

4. ANTENNA: Cut a length of color B approximately 1" (2.5 cm) long. Fold the strand in half and thread it partway through 1 stitch on top of the Snail's head. Insert the loose ends of the folded strand through the folded end and pull tight. Trim the ends, if desired.

MARBLED SCARVES
AND HANDKERCHIEFS

WITH ILANA KOHN + EMILY EIBEL

The technique of marbling has been used for centuries to decorate surfaces with swirling patterns, much like the patterns that naturally exist in marble stone. I was captivated the first time I saw the beautifully detailed and boldly graphic silk scarves in Ilana's eponymous clothing line, made together by Ilana and Emily. Part of marbling's appeal is that each print is completely unique—though this can also be a source of frustration if you are trying to reproduce a print you've already made! Ilana and Emily have learned to simply go with the flow and let the process guide them (often with spectacular results), and hopefully your process will follow suit.

Note: If you are making scarves it is best to do this project with a friend so you can each hold two corners of the fabric as you lower it onto the surface of the marbling bath. For handkerchiefs, one pair of hands is enough. Silk is ideal for marbling because of its smooth surface, but other finely woven fabrics made from natural fibers will work well, too.

MATERIALS:

Plastic bucket, large enough to submerge your fabric

Rubber gloves (optional)

Apron (optional)

Alum (pure aluminum sulphate)*

1-quart (1-L) container (a clean, empty yogurt container works well)**

Measuring cups**

Whisk and mixing spoon**

Silk scraps for testing

Silk habotai handkerchiefs or scarves

Plastic drop cloth

Iron

Fluid water-based fabric paint, such as Jacquard Dye-Na-Flow silk paint, in colors of your choice

6- or 8-ounce (170- or 235-ml) plastic dropper/squeeze bottle, one for each color of paint

Foil roasting pan or plastic bin, slightly larger than your handkerchief or scarf size

Measuring spoons**

Methocel (also called methyl cellulose or methylcel)

Non-sudsing household ammonia

Old newspapers

*It is important that the alum is pure aluminum sulphate; do not use alum containing potassium, ammonium, or anything else, since these extra chemicals may harm your fabric.

**Not to be used again for food

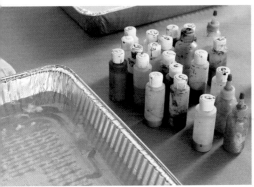

A) Prep fabric paint bottles   *B) If paint sinks, more methocel is needed*   *C) Bath is ready when paint floats*

1. SET UP AND SAFETY: You will need a work area of approximately 4' x 6' (1.2 m x 1.8 m) for marbling handkerchiefs and 8' x 10' (2.5 m x 3 m) for marbling scarves, on a table or on the floor. The safety concerns with marbling are very minimal. Alum is a chemical compound used for many purposes—from purifying water to making deodorant to pickling vegetables—but it tends to dry out the skin, so wash your hands after using it, or wear gloves. Avoid inhaling the dry alum dust, which can irritate your nose. Methocel is nontoxic and used in many food products as a thickener. Ammonia should never be mixed with any liquid containing bleach, or a poisonous gas may result. Water-based fabric paint is considered nontoxic, but as with any dyeing or printing project, work in a well-ventilated area. Wear an apron if you wish to protect your clothes.

2. SOAK FABRIC IN ALUM BATH: Using a 1 quart (1-L) container, fill the bucket with enough room-temperature water to submerge your fabric, keeping track of how many quarts of water you add (4 quarts or liters equal 1 gallon). Add ¼ cup (60 ml) of alum per gallon of water and stir with the whisk. Soak your scarves, handkerchiefs, and test fabric in the alum mixture for 90 minutes and then lay them out to dry on the plastic drop cloth. Note that alum acts as a color binder (or mordant), fixing the colors to the fabric permanently. But it is corrosive and will eat away at fabric if left too long, so you will need to marble your fabric within 2 days of soaking it in the alum mixture. Wash the bucket with soap and water.

3. PREPARE FABRIC AND PAINT: Allow the fabric to dry completely, then iron it well. Any wet areas will not take paint and any wrinkled areas will appear in the final print. Set the dry, pressed fabric aside, stacked on a large, flat surface.

Pour the fabric paint into the plastic droppers or bottles. Paint can be mixed to create new colors, if desired. Mix small amounts first so that you don't waste paint if you mix a color you do not like *(A)*.

4. PREPARE MARBLING BATH: Set the foil pan or plastic bin on your work surface. Use your 1-quart (1-L) container to fill the foil roasting pan or plastic bin with approximately 3" (7.5 cm) of room-temperature water, keeping track of how many quarts are used (4 quarts or liters equal 1 gallon). Add 2 tablespoons of methocel per gallon of water. Stir well with a spoon. Add 1 teaspoon of ammonia per gallon of water and stir again. Wait 10 minutes and stir again. Wait another 10 to 15

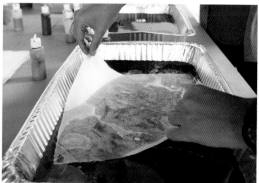

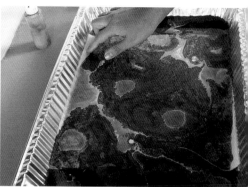

D) Squeeze droplets of paint on bath   *E) Gently place fabric on bath*   *F) Let fabric lay entirely on surface*

minutes, then test the bath to make sure the paint will float properly on the surface by squeezing a drop or two of paint into the bath and observing whether it floats. If it sinks and leaves a tadpole-like trail *(B)*, more methocel is necessary (add 1 tablespoon more, wait, then test again). If the paint floats and spreads across the surface of the bath *(C)*, the bath is ready for marbling. Fill the bucket you used for the alum with 3" to 4" (7.5 cm to 10 cm) of cold water and set it to the side.

5. APPLY PAINT TO SURFACE OF MARBLING BATH: Choose the color you want to start with and hold the plastic bottle vertically over the bath. Gently drop paint onto the bath one drop at a time. Hold the bottle approximately 6" (15 cm) from the surface to ensure that the paint droplets will not break the surface tension of the water and simply sink to the bottom. Though some will end up sinking to the bottom of the bath, the goal is to get as much of the paint to remain on the surface as possible since this is what will ultimately be printed on the fabric. Continue squeezing drops of paint with other colors of your choice *(D)*.

At this point, you should see "stones" (round paint spots) appear where the paint is sitting on the surface of the bath. Marbling is an unpredictable process and you may not always get nice round spots due to many factors, like pH balance and temperature. When you are not seeing these nice, round spots on the surface of the water, go through the steps again and troubleshoot. Did you mix the bath properly? Is the paint too thick? Certain colors will behave differently, depending on the other paints used and the order in which they were applied. If you aren't getting the look you planned, embrace what is working and go with it!

If you would like to have more control over the way your paint appears on the surface of the bath, here are some techniques to try:

THREAD TECHNIQUE: Gently drag a piece of thread through the paint to break it up and move it around a bit.

COMB TECHNIQUE: To achieve featherlike shapes, create a small comb tool by taping toothpicks, evenly spaced, to a wooden paint mixing stick. Gently drag the tool through the paint.

EMPTY-BOTTLE TECHNIQUE: Use a bottle of paint that is almost empty to squirt air on the surface of the bath and move the paint around.

G) Pick up fabric at 2 corners

H) Place marbled fabric in water bucket

I) Clean surface of bath with newspaper

SUMINAGASHI TECHNIQUE: A Japanese marbling technique where drops of paint are placed within the center of the previous drop over and over creating concentric rings like a tree trunk. Try shaking the pan a bit when done to distort the rings.

POLLOCK TECHNIQUE: Simply squirt paint all over like Jackson Pollock (being somewhat gentle—you don't want too much of the paint to sink).

6. MARBLE FABRIC: You may want to test the colors and patterns on scrap fabric before printing on your silk handkerchief or scarf. Fabric that is 12" (30 cm) square or smaller can be placed on the surface of the bath by one person, but larger pieces of fabric should be done with 2 sets of hands. With clean fingers, pick up the fabric at 2 opposite corners and let the fabric hang in a U shape. Gently place the fabric on the surface of the bath, starting at the center of the U *(E)*, and then drop down the sides until it lays entirely on the surface of the bath *(F)*. Tap down on any air bubbles under the fabric. You will see the fabric absorb the marbled paint. Pick up the fabric at 2 corners *(G)* and place it directly into the water bucket *(H)*. Gently rinse the fabric and then hang it to dry. Repeat Steps 5 and 6 using a new piece of fabric.

7. CLEAR SURFACE OF BATH: Stop to clean the surface of the bath every few prints or when you want to change the colors. Fold a piece of newspaper into a long, narrow rectangle. Drag the newspaper along the surface of the bath from top to bottom, gently skimming off the paint (this will remove some paint from the surface and force some paint below the surface) *(I)*. Keep in mind that the paint you still see below the surface of the bath will remain there and will not affect your next print. Discard the newspaper and apply paint as in Step 5.

8. FINISH: Pour the marbling bath and bucket of water down the drain. Once the handkerchiefs are dry, iron them thoroughly on their unprinted sides to set the paint. Wait a few days before washing the scarves by hand, to be sure the paint has thoroughly set.

In Ilana and Emily's class, students typically begin slowly, hesitant about which colors to choose. With some encouragement, the students dive in, and in no time they are lifting their first handkerchiefs from the marbling bath. The results are thrilling!

FREEFORM KNITTED THROW

WITH ERIN WECKERLE

The first time I went into Erin's Brooklyn shop I noticed the chandelier hanging from the ceiling—she had covered almost all of the brass with a crocheted cozy. Having done some unconventional crocheting myself, I immediately felt that Erin was a kindred spirit. When discussing projects for the book, Erin and I wanted to do a knitted throw with the feeling of a freeform scrap quilt. This throw project begins at the center and grows out in a loose, organic manner. All of the yarns used for the throw should be the same gauge, but the texture and fiber content can be different. The stitch pattern we used for the throw—seed stitch—is a simple pattern that alternates between one knit stitch and one purl stitch, creating a wonderful, nubby texture that won't roll at the edges. Erin sketched a rough plan for the quilt blocks beforehand and you can do the same, or you can simply add blocks to the blanket as you go. (If you are new to knitting, be sure to check out the knitting basics on page 169.)

FINISHED MEASUREMENTS

Approximately 36" (90 cm) square

YARN

12 to 18 hanks worsted weight 100% wool yarn in a variety of colors (the blanket on the facing page used 16 yarn colors; approximately 175 to 250 yards / 160 to 229 meters per color)

NEEDLES

One pair straight needles size US 10 (6 mm) (change needle size if necessary to obtain correct gauge)

NOTIONS

Crochet hook size I/9 (5.5 mm) (optional)
Tapestry needle

GAUGE

16 stitches and 24 rows = 4" (10 cm) in Seed Stitch

A) Changing to a different color

B) Picking up stitches

C) Backward loop cast-on

STITCH PATTERN

Seed Stitch (even number of stitches; 2-row repeat)

ROW 1: *Knit 1, purl 1; repeat from * to end.

ROW 2: *Purl 1, knit 1; repeat from * to end.

Repeat Rows 1 and 2 for Seed Stitch (even number of stitches).

Seed Stitch (odd number of stitches; 1-row repeat)

ALL ROWS: Knit 1, *purl 1, knit 1; repeat from * to end.

1. START THE THROW: If you want to pre-plan the look of your Throw, try sketching a few color-blocking ideas. The design for my Throw began by determining the size of one of the central blocks; this block became the base to which I anchored the other blocks.

Cast on the desired number of stitches for the central block. To determine how many stitches to cast on, you can multiply the desired width of the block by 4 (the number of stitches per inch), then cast on the resulting number. Work in Seed stitch (for even or odd number of stitches, depending on how many you cast on) until block is the desired length. At this point, you may either change to a different color or bind off all the stitches.

2. START A NEW BLOCK: When you want to add a new block to the Throw, you have 3 choices for how to do it. The simplest way is to just continue to work in the same direction on an existing block that is already on the needles, but change colors *(A)*. The next easiest is to pick up and knit stitches along the edge of an existing block (see page 173) *(B)*. Or you can start a fresh block by casting on stitches with a new color and working the block as you did for the first block, then sew or join the new block to other blocks after it's completed.

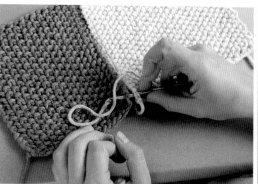

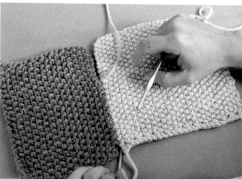

D) An extended block   *E) Use crochet hook to join two blocks*   *F) Two joined blocks*

If you're working on existing stitches that are already on the needle, and you want to extend one end of the block or the other, you can cast on additional stitches on the end that you want to extend, using the Backward Loop Cast-On Method *(C)*. Once you have cast on the additional stitches, continue working rows *(D)*.

3. FINISH THROW: Your Throw will grow as you continue adding blocks. When you have reached the edge of the Throw or are ready to finish a block, bind off that section. When you are happy with the overall shape and layout of the color blocks, go back and sew (using a tapestry needle) or join (using a crochet hook) *(E + F)* together any blocks that are still unattached, using yarn in a matching color to hide the seam, or in a contrasting color to accentuate the seam. Using a tapestry needle, weave in any loose ends.

CROCHETED GARLAND

WITH ERIN WECKERLE

I met Erin seven years ago at her shop, Sodafine. I was excited to have a store so close to my new home in Brooklyn that was stocked with clothing and other handmade goods from independent designers. Erin sold her own pieces, too, including intricately crocheted jewelry and knitted winter hats. For this project, Erin used three different doily patterns to create a garland and chose a muted, antiquelike color palette so the garland wouldn't feel too childish. Most of the doilies shown here are worked in a single color, though you can also work the final round in a different color (see examples on page 130). The garland can be strung up anywhere year-round, and would look great on a mantel, a window frame, or a headboard. The slight sheen of the linen yarn adds to the grown-up look of this garland, though other yarn types would work well, too. If you do use linen, Erin recommends working with steel crochet hooks instead of plastic because of the way the linen yarn glides along them.

MATERIALS:

Euroflax Sport Weight Linen* (100% wet spun linen; 270 yards / 247 m; 100 grams): 1 hank each in colors Champagne, Goldilocks, Natural, and Pewter

*You may substitute a linen of your choice; just make sure to use a yarn with a gauge of 6 stitches per inch (2.5 cm)

One size B/C/1 (2.25 mm) crochet hook

One size F/5 (3.75 mm) crochet hook

Scissors

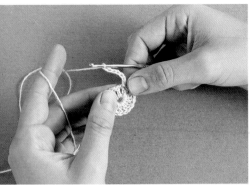

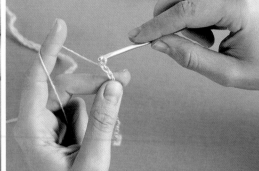

A) Start Round 2 by chaining 8   *B) Round 2*   *C) Create chain*

1. LARGE DOILY

Note: For basic crochet instructions, see page 173.

With the smaller crochet hook, chain 6 and slip stitch into first chain to join into a ring.

ROUND 1: Chain 3 to create first double crochet. Work 15 additional double crochet into center of ring. Join with a slip stitch to the top of first chain 3, for a total of 16 double crochet.

ROUND 2: *Chain 8 *(A)*. Slip stitch into the next double crochet; repeat from * 14 more times *(B)*. To finish the round, chain 4 and treble crochet into base of first chain 8 for a total of 16 loops.

ROUND 3: Chain 3 to create first double crochet. Double crochet once in same chain space, 2 double crochet in next chain space, and chain 2. *2 double crochet in next chain space, 2 double crochet in next chain space, and chain 2*; repeat from * to * around to the beginning. Join with a slip stitch to the top of the first chain 3, for a total of 32 double crochet.

ROUND 4: Slip stitch across to next chain 2 space. Chain 3, (2 double crochet, chain 2, and 3 double crochet) in same chain space. *Chain 2, (3 double crochet, chain 2, 3 double crochet) in next chain 2 space*; repeat from * to * around to the beginning. Chain 1, single crochet in the top of first chain 3 to join, for a total of 8 shells.

ROUND 5: Single crochet in same chain space. *Chain 10, skip next 6 double crochet shell, and single crochet in next chain 2 space between shells*; repeat from * to * around to last chain space. Chain 5, treble crochet in first single crochet to join, for a total of 9 loops.

ROUND 6: (Single crochet, 2 half-double crochet, 2 double crochet, 2 treble crochet) in same chain space. *(2 treble crochet, 2 double crochet, 2 half-double crochet, 1 single crochet, 2 half-double crochet, 2 double crochet, 2 treble crochet) in next chain space.* Repeat from * to *, ending with (2 treble crochet, 2 double crochet, 2 half-double crochet) in starting chain space. Join with a slip stitch to top of first single crochet.

Repeat to make 3 more large doilies.

2. MEDIUM DOILY

With the smaller crochet hook, chain 8 and slip stitch into first chain to join into a ring.

ROUND 1: Chain 3 (for first double crochet). Work 15 additional double crochet into ring. Slip stitch to top of first chain 3, for a total of 16 double crochet.

ROUND 2: Chain 3. Double crochet once in same stitch. Continue around making 2 double crochet in each stitch. Slip stitch to top of first chain 3, for a total of 32 double crochet.

ROUND 3: Chain 5. Skip first 2 stitches. Double crochet in next double crochet, chain 2. *Skip a stitch, double crochet in next double crochet, and chain 2*; repeat from * to * around to the beginning. Slip stitch to top of first chain 3 to join, for a total of 16 double crochet.

ROUND 4: Slip stitch into first chain 2 space. Chain 3, 3 double crochet in same chain space, chain 1. *4 double crochet in next chain 2 space, chain 1*; repeat from * to * around. Slip stitch to top of first chain 3 to join, for a total of 60 double crochet.

ROUND 5: *Chain 5, skip next 4 double crochet shell, and single crochet into next chain space*; repeat from * to * around. Slip stitch to first chain to join, for a total of 15 loops.

ROUND 6: Slip stitch into first loop. Chain 2, (half-double crochet, 2 double crochet) in first loop, chain 1, *(2 half-double crochet, 2 double crochet) in next loop, chain 1*; repeat from * to * around. Slip stitch to top of first chain 2 to join, for a total of 75 stitches.

Repeat to make 3 more medium doilies.

3. SMALL DOILY

With the smaller crochet hook, chain 8 and slip stitch into first chain to join into a ring.

ROUND 1: Chain 4 (counts as double crochet, chain 1). *Double crochet in next chain, chain 1*; repeat from * to * around to the beginning. Slip stitch to top of first chain 3 to join, for a total of 9 double crochet.

ROUND 2: Slip stitch into first chain space, chain 3, 2 double crochet in same chain space, chain 1. *3 double crochet in next chain space, chain 1*; repeat from * to * around. Slip stitch to top of first double crochet to join, for a total of 27 double crochet.

ROUND 3: Slip stitch 3 stitches to next chain space, chain 3, 3 double crochet in same chain space, chain 2. *4 double crochet in next chain space, chain 2*; repeat from * to * around. Slip stitch to top of first double crochet to join, for a total of 36 double crochet.

ROUND 4: Slip stitch 4 stitches to next chain space, chain 3, 4 double crochet in same chain space, chain 3. *5 double crochet in next chain space, chain 3*; repeat from * to * around. Slip stitch to top of the first double crochet to join, for a total of 45 double crochet.

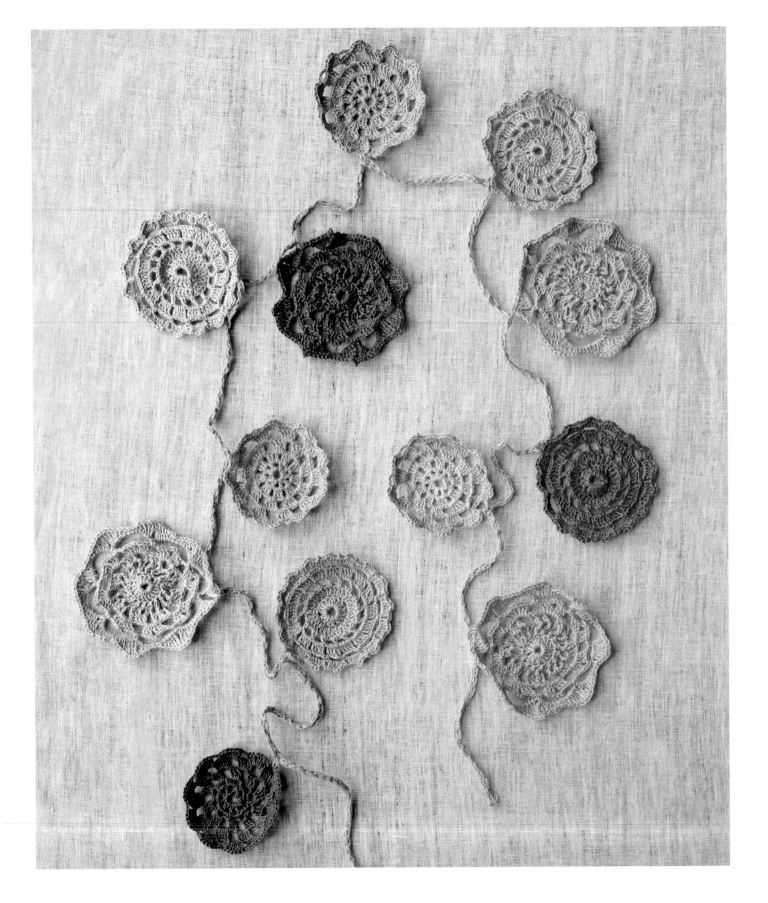

*D) Pick up doily every
15 to 20 stitches*

*E) Attach chain to doily
with single crochet*

F) Erin attaches doilies to a chain

ROUND 5: Slip stitch 5 stitches to next chain space. (Chain 2, 1 half-double crochet, 2 double crochet, 2 half-double crochet) in next chain space, chain 3. *(2 half-double crochet, 2 double crochet, 2 half-double crochet), chain 3*; repeat from * to * around. Slip stitch to top of first half-double crochet to join, for a total of 9 shells.

Repeat to make 3 more small doilies.

4. CREATE THE GARLAND

With the larger crochet hook, create a chain 6' to 8' (1.8 m to 2.5 m) long *(C)*.

Turn. Single crochet into each stitch, picking up a doily every 15 to 20 stitches *(D)* and attaching with a single crochet stitch *(E + F)*.

TIE-DYED PILLOWCASES

WITH SHABD SIMON-ALEXANDER

The first time I saw Shabd Simon-Alexander's striking tie-dyed clothing, it gave me a whole new appreciation for this dyeing technique. Shabd's fine art background is evident in her work, which is inspired by both modern expressionist art and folk traditions. Her classes in my studio were always very popular, and we couldn't keep up with the demand.

There are many ways you can fold fabric when tie-dyeing, but for these pillowcases we decided to use loose folds and string to achieve soft waves across the fabric. Even with years of experience, tie-dye results can still be a surprise to Shabd—and that is part of the fun. It's best to keep an open mind about your end result and enjoy the imperfect nature of the process.

MATERIALS:

Plastic drop cloth

Apron (optional)

Rubber gloves (optional)

Dust mask (optional)

2 white pillowcases, washed and dried (cotton works best, but any natural fabric like silk, rayon, linen, or hemp will work)

String or twine

Scissors

Two 1-quart (1-L) containers (clean, empty yogurt containers work well)*

Two buckets or plastic bins (large enough to fit your pillowcases, plus room to swish around)*

¼-cup (32-g) dry measuring cup*

Soda ash

Whisk or spoon*

Measuring spoons*

⅔-ounce (19-g) jar of Procion MX dye, in color of your choice

Noniodized salt (optional)

16-ounce (480-ml) liquid measuring cup (optional)

Paper towel or scrap fabric (optional)

Scissors (optional)

Mild dish soap or laundry detergent

*Not to be used again for food

A) Wrap string around fabric

B) Wrap entire pillowcase

C) Immerse pillowcase

1. SET UP AND SAFETY: You will need a work surface of approximately 4' x 6' (1.2 m x 1.8 m). Cover your work surface with a plastic drop cloth. Wear an apron if you wish to protect your clothes. The safety concerns with tie-dyeing are minimal, but dyes and soda ash should not be inhaled and soda ash can irritate the skin, so you may want to wear rubber gloves and a dust mask when mixing them. As with any dyeing or printing project, work in a well-ventilated area.

2. TIE PILLOWCASES: Lay a pillowcase on your work surface. Start at one short end of the pillowcase and scrunch the width of the fabric together. To achieve a loosely dyed appearance, do not fold the fabric neatly, but instead bunch it together in an uneven fashion. Cut a length of string approximately 6' (1.8 m) long and knot it around the bunched fabric. Begin to wrap the string around and around the fabric *(A)*, sometimes close together and sometimes farther apart. As you continue down the length of the pillowcase, scrunching the fabric and wrapping it with string, rearrange the folds of the fabric so that different areas will be more exposed to dye. Areas that are more densely wrapped will have more white space in the finished result, and areas that are more loosely wrapped will have more color. When you reach the end of the pillowcase, knot the string and cut off any extra *(B)*. Repeat with the second pillowcase.

Note: You can experiment with wrapping the fabric any way you like. More precise accordion folds, for example, will likely result in a more uniform pattern.

3. PRESOAK PILLOWCASES: Presoaking fabric in a soda ash solution allows the dyes to bond permanently to the fibers of the fabric. Using a 1-quart (1-L) container, fill one bucket with enough hot water to submerge your pillowcases, keeping track of how many quarts you use (4 quarts or liters equal 1 gallon). Mix in ¼ cup (32 g) of soda ash per quart (liter) of water. Mix with the whisk or spoon until all of the soda ash dissolves. Soak the pillowcases in this mixture for 30 minutes.

4. MIX DYES: While your pillowcases are soaking, fill the other bucket with enough lukewarm water to submerge your pillowcases with room to swish around, then prepare your dye bath. Keep track of how many quarts (liters) of water you use to fill your bucket, and calculate the amount of dye needed following the instructions on the package. You may wish to fully dissolve the dye

D) Cut string   *E) Unravel pillowcase*   *F) Shabd with finished pillowcase*

granules in a smaller amount of water before adding it to the rest of the water in the dye bucket. If so, use a 1-quart (1 L) container to initially mix the dye, and then pour the dissolved dye into the bucket.

Adding noniodized salt to your dye bath will help yield a deeper, richer color. Check the instructions on the dye package for the amount of salt needed, and dissolve the salt in approximately 2 cups (480 ml) of hot water before adding it to the dye bath.

To get an idea of the finished color, dip a paper towel or piece of scrap fabric in the dye bath and blot it onto a clean paper or cloth. The blotted color will be a close representation of the finished dye color. Adjust the ratio of water to dye depending on the color you want. Remember that colors always appear a bit lighter on dry fabric than on wet fabric.

5. DYE PILLOWCASES: Remove the pillowcases from the soda ash solution and wring out excess liquid. Immerse your pillowcases in the dye bath *(C)* and let them soak for 1 hour, occasionally swishing to ensure an even application. After an hour, remove the pillowcases and wring out excess liquid.

6. RINSE PILLOWCASES: Rinse the pillowcases in cold water until the water runs clear, then remove the strings *(D + E + F)*. Machine-wash or hand wash the pillowcases in hot water with a mild detergent to remove any excess dye. Line- or machine-dry the pillowcases.

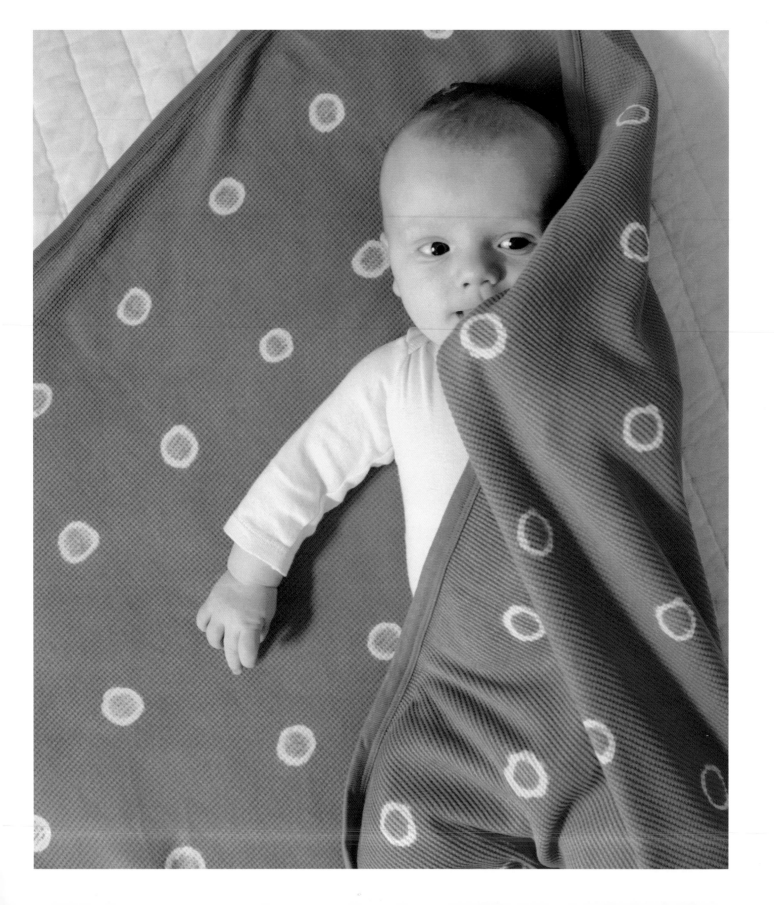

TIE-DYED BABY BLANKET

WITH SHABD SIMON-ALEXANDER

Shabd's tie-dyeing classes in my studio were pure fun. From wrapping and tying the fabric to dipping the clean pieces into the dye bath to the excitement of unveiling the finished goods, students were always eager to get started and then giddy upon revealing their tie-dyed pieces at the very end.

To make the rings on this baby blanket, you lay a spherical shape on the fabric and snugly tie the object within the blanket. When Shabd and I developed this project at her Brooklyn studio, we brainstormed and experimented with different objects to create the rings. I had brought a variety of balls and marbles, but we found we wanted something smaller. Dried kidney beans nearly worked, but their shapes were too irregular, and lentils were too small. As it turned out, dried chickpeas were just right, and we wrapped them into the blanket with small rubber bands. (If you want less precise rings, you can tie them in loosely with string.)

MATERIALS:

Plastic drop cloth

Apron (optional)

Dust mask (optional)

Rubber gloves (optional)

100% cotton (or other natural fabric, such as linen, hemp, or silk) cream-colored baby blanket, washed and dried

Water-soluble (disappearing-ink) fabric pen

Ruler (optional)

Dried chickpeas*

Small rubber bands

Soda ash

Two 1-quart (1-L) containers (clean, empty yogurt containers work well)*

Two buckets or plastic bins, 5 gallons or larger (large enough for your blanket to fit with room to swish around)*

1/4-cup (32-g) dry measuring cup*

Whisk or spoon*

Measuring spoons*

2/3-ounce (19-g) jar of Procion MX dye, in color of your choice

Noniodized salt (optional)

16-ounce (480-ml) liquid measuring cup (optional)

Paper towel or scrap fabric (optional)

Scissors (optional)

Mild dish soap or laundry detergent

*Not to be used again for food

A) Mark placement of circles   *B) Tie chickpeas inside blanket*   *C) Measure dye*

1. SET UP: You will need a work surface of approximately 4' x 6' (1.2 m x 1.8 m). Wear an apron if you wish to protect your clothes, and cover your work surface with a plastic drop cloth. Dyes and soda ash should not be inhaled, and soda ash can irritate the skin, so you might want to wear a dust mask and rubber gloves when mixing them. As with any dyeing or printing project, work in a well-ventilated area.

2. TIE KNOTS: Lay the dry blanket on your work surface. Using the water-soluble pen, mark the spots on the blanket where you would like to place the circles *(A)*. This can be done loosely by hand, or with a ruler for more precise results. For the blanket on page 136, the circles are approximately 5" (12.5 cm) apart.

Place a chickpea beneath the blanket at each marked spot. Grasp each chickpea from above, through the blanket, and wrap a rubber band around the fabric with the chickpea inside *(B)*. Continue until a chickpea has been wrapped beneath all the marked spots.

3. PRESOAK BLANKET: Presoaking fabric in a soda ash solution allows the dyes to bond permanently to the fibers of the fabric. Using a 1-quart (1-L) container, fill one bucket with enough hot water to submerge your blanket, keeping track of how many quarts of water you use (4 quarts or liters equal 1 gallon). Mix in ¼ cup (32 g) of soda ash per quart (liter) of water. Mix with the whisk or spoon until all of the soda ash dissolves. Soak your blanket in this mixture for 30 minutes.

4. MIX DYES: While your blanket is soaking, fill the other bucket with enough lukewarm water to submerge your blanket with room to swish around, then prepare your dye bath. Keep track of how many quarts (liters) of water you use to fill the bucket, and calculate the amount of dye needed following the instructions on the package *(C)*.

You may wish to fully dissolve the dye granules in a smaller amount of water before adding it to the rest of the water in the dye bucket. If so, use a 1-quart (1-L) container to initially mix the dye *(D)*, and then pour the dissolved dye into the bucket *(E + F)*.

Adding noniodized salt to your dye bath will help yield a deeper, richer color. Check the instructions on the dye package for the amount of salt needed and dissolve the salt in approximately 2 cups (480 ml) of hot water before adding it to the dye bath.

D) Dissolve dye

E) Shabd mixing dye bath

F) Pour dissolved dye into bucket

G) Submerge blanket in dye

H) Swish around

*I) Remove rubber bands
and chickpeas*

To get an idea of the finished color of your dye, dip a paper towel or piece of scrap fabric in the dye bath and blot it onto a clean paper or cloth. The blotted color will be a close representation of the finished dye color. Adjust the ratio of water to dye depending on the color you want. Remember that colors always appear a bit lighter on dry fabric than on wet fabric.

5. DYE BLANKET: Remove the blanket from the soda ash solution and wring out excess liquid. Immerse the blanket in the dye bath *(G + H)* and let it soak for 1 hour, occasionally swishing the blanket around in the dye to ensure an even application. After an hour, remove the blanket and wring out excess liquid.

6. FINISH BLANKET: Rinse the blanket in cold water until the water runs clear. Remove the rubber bands and chickpeas; it may be helpful to use scissors to cut off the rubber bands *(I)*, but be very careful to not snip the blanket. Machine-wash or handwash the blanket in hot water with a mild detergent to remove any excess dye. Machine- or line-dry the blanket.

SEWN AND STUFFED TOYS

WITH SIAN KEEGAN

I met Sian while she was studying surface design at The Fashion Institute of Technology, and it has been a pleasure watching her career as an independent designer and craftperson flourish since then. I have seen photographs of Sian's whimsical, three-dimensional creations taken by her customers from places as far away as Paris and Tokyo. Over the years, her stuffed-and-sewn designs have taken the shape of dogs, bears, bunnies, narwhals, and even potted plants and bunches of scallions, but my favorites have always been her strawberries and radishes. I particularly love how they look in a group, with each one slightly different because of the fabric combinations she chooses. Sian sews her toys both on a machine and by hand with a needle and thread (though they could be sewn entirely by hand, if you prefer). Machine-sewing the small pieces requires focus and patience at first, but will go rather quickly once you get the hang of it. The sewing required to close up the form and add leaves and stems is all done by hand. As Sian says, any evidence of hand stitching serves as a charming reminder that the piece is handmade.

MATERIALS:

Tracing paper

Pencil

Paper scissors

Approximately ¼ yard (¼ m) each of 4 quilting-weight cotton fabrics, in shades of dark red, red, pink, and cream

Straight pins

Fabric scissors

Sewing machine

Red and green thread

Stuffing (cotton, wool, or kapok works best)

Hand-sewing needle

18" (45 cm) green yarn for strawberry stems

Approximately ¼ yard (¼ m) green felt, in different prints, if desired

Ruler

Embroidery needle

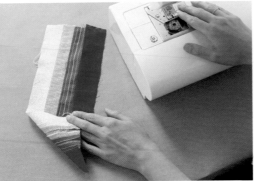

A) Cut strips of fabric *B) Sew strips together* *C) Cut out Radish pattern pieces*

RADISH

1. CUT OUT PATTERNS: Lay a piece of tracing paper over the radish templates on pages 166 and 167 and trace them with a pencil. Cut the pieces from the tracing paper and label them.

2. CREATE PATCHWORK: Cut a 12" (30 cm)-long strip of each of the 4 cotton fabrics in the following widths: 2" (5-cm)-wide dark red fabric; 1¾" (4.5-cm)-wide red fabric; 1½" (4-cm)-wide pink fabric; and 1½" (4-cm)-wide cream fabric *(A)*.

With right sides facing and the long edges aligned, sew together the cream and pink strips with a ⅜" (10 mm) seam allowance. Next, align the long edges of the red strip with the pink strip, with right sides facing, and sew them together with a ⅜" (10 mm) seam allowance. Repeat to attach the dark red strip to the red strip *(B)*. Press the seams open.

Cut the 12" (36-cm)-long patchwork piece into 4 equal sections, each 3" (7.5 cm) long. Stack two of the patchwork pieces on top of each other, facing the same direction, and pin the Radish pattern piece to them. Cut around the shape *(C)*. Make small notches at the top and bottom edges (as indicated on the pattern piece) to mark the center. Repeat with the other two patchwork pieces.

3. CUT AND SEW LEAVES: Pin the Radish Leaf patterns to the green felt and cut out five pieces, as noted on the patterns. Using green thread, stitch down the center of each leaf in one continuous pass *(D)*. Snip the thread connecting the leaves.

4. ASSEMBLE RADISH: Lay one of the Radish pieces on a work surface, right side facing up. Align the bases of 2 leaves with the top of the Radish piece (as indicated by the arrow on the pattern). Pin the pieces together and sew them in place with ¼" (6 mm) seam allowance *(E)*. Repeat with the other three Radish pieces, but sewing just one leaf to each.

Lay two of the Radish pieces on top of each other, with right sides facing and patchwork seams aligned. Sew the edges of the two pieces together with a ⅜" (10 mm) seam allowance, sewing from one notch to the other. Repeat this step to join the third and fourth pieces, leaving a 1¼" (3 cm) opening at the top.

D) Stitch down center of each leaf   *E) Sew leaves to Radish pieces*   *F) Hand-sew opening closed*

5. FINISH RADISH: Trim the seams and turn the Radish right-side out through the opening, pulling the leaves out. Tear off small pieces of stuffing and stuff the Radish densely. Use the eraser end of a pencil to push in the filling. Stitch the opening closed by hand with a blind stitch (see *Fig. 2* on page 147) *(F)*.

STRAWBERRY

1. CUT OUT PATTERNS: Lay a piece of tracing paper over the strawberry templates on page 167 and trace them with a pencil. Cut the pieces from the tracing paper and label them.

2. CUT STRAWBERRY FABRIC: Layer the 4 cotton fabrics on top of one another and pin the Strawberry pattern to the stacked fabric. Using fabric scissors, cut through all four pieces of fabric at once. Make a small notch at the top and bottom of each piece (as indicated on the pattern piece) to mark the exact center of each piece.

Pin the Strawberry Stem pattern piece to the green felt and cut it out using fabric scissors.

3. ASSEMBLE STRAWBERRY: Lay two of the Strawberry pieces together, with right sides facing and edges aligned. Sew along one half of the Strawberry from notch to notch, with a ³⁄₈" (10 mm) seam allowance. Repeat this step to join the third and fourth pieces, making sure the right sides of each piece of fabric are facing and edges are aligned. Leave a 1" (2.5 cm) opening at the top.

4. FINISH STRAWBERRY: Trim the seams and turn the Strawberry right-side out. Tear off small pieces of stuffing and stuff the Strawberry densely. Use the eraser end of a pencil to push in the filling. Stitch the opening closed by hand with a blind stitch (see *Fig. 2* on page 147).

For the stem, thread a 4" (10 cm) length of green yarn through the embroidery needle. Tie a knot at one end of the yarn, pull the needle through the center of the felt Strawberry Stem, and cut the yarn to approximately 1¼" (3 cm).

Thread a hand-sewing needle with a length of green thread; pull the thread through the needle to the midpoint to double it and knot the end. Sew a running stitch (see *Fig. 1* on page 147) in a circle around the stem to attach the base of the Strawberry Stem to the Strawberry (but keep the edges of the leaves loose).

PATCHWORK PILLOW

WITH SIAN KEEGAN

Sian's first memory of creating patchwork was when she was in the Girl Scouts. Each scout was given a bag of precut squares and triangles of fabric, and they stitched the pieces together by hand to start a quilt. Now, as Sian works on patchwork projects, she tosses any fabric scraps larger than a postcard into a large bin. Added to the mix are bits of excess fabric that her friends with fashion and textile jobs give her, so her collection of scraps is a surprising mix of patterns and textures. For this project, she used a selection of "ditsy" patterned fabric in a tonal color palette inspired by feed-sack bags from the 1930s and 1940s. You may want to choose a pleasing combination of new fabric as we did here, or start collecting remnants from other projects in a bin for future patchwork use.

MATERIALS:

½ yard (½ m) muslin fabric (or quilting-weight cotton or linen fabric), washed and dried

½ yard (½ m) each of 5 quilting-weight cotton fabrics, washed and dried

Measuring tape

Fabric scissors

Straight pins

Iron

Thread in a neutral color, similar in tone to the patterned fabrics

Hand-sewing needle or sewing machine

18" (45-cm)-square down (or faux down) pillow insert

Spray bottle filled with water (optional)

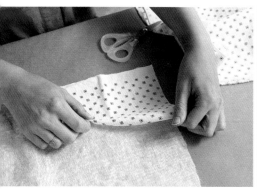

A) Cut and place first patchwork piece   *B) Pin patchwork in place*   *C) Continue adding patchwork*

1. CUT FRONT AND BACK FABRICS: Measure and cut two 18" (45 cm) squares of muslin. Place one square in the center of your work surface and set the other aside.

2. PLAN PATCHWORK: For this method of patchwork, the pieces will not be sewn to one another, but arranged in an overlapping pattern and sewn to the muslin backing. Before you start cutting fabrics for the patchwork, you might find it helpful to look at the patchwork design on page 144, or sketch ideas until you're pleased with the layout of the shapes.

Pieces can be cut with both straight angles and curves. You may find it easiest to cut a patchwork piece for each corner and then fill in the center, or you may prefer working from one side to the other; both techniques work well. Two sides of each corner piece will need to be straight, to form a right angle.

Choose a piece of patterned fabric for the first shape, and cut it to a size and shape of your choice *(A)*. Iron the edge(s) of the patchwork piece ¼" (6 mm) to the wrong side; note that any edges that touch the outer edge of the square do not need to be turned under, as the outer edges will be sewn into the seams of the pillow. To iron a crisp, folded edge, spray the fabric with water before ironing. Pin the piece to the muslin with several straight pins.

The second piece of patchwork can either slide under the edge of the first piece or sit on top of it. Cut the second piece. Fold and press ¼" (6 mm) to the wrong side any edges that will overlap another piece, and pin the shape in place to the muslin backing. Continue cutting patchwork pieces one at a time, ironing the edges that will overlap, and pinning the pieces to the muslin *(B + C)*. You can play with the layout of the patchwork by unpinning pieces and moving or recutting shapes, if desired. When the square is entirely filled with patchwork pieces, add extra pins (especially along the perimeter) to ensure that the patchwork stays secure when moved.

D) Hand-sew starting at edge   *E) Use a straight stitch to hand-sew*   *F) Sian hand-sews her pillowcase*

3. SEW PATCHWORK: The patchwork can be sewn by hand or machine.

HAND-SEWING: Thread the needle with a long length of thread, pulling it through to the mid-point to double it. Knot the strands together at the end. Starting at the outside of the pillow, sew along the overlapping edges of the patchwork pieces with a straight stitch *(D + E + F; Fig. 1)*. Remove the pins as you sew, and tie a knot on the wrong side of the fabric when you reach the end of a length of thread. Continue sewing all of the seams this way.

MACHINE-SEWING: Using a stitch length between 2 and 4, sew along the overlapping edges of each patchwork piece, removing the pins as you sew.

4. SEW PILLOW: Lay the patchwork and the second 18" (45-cm)-square piece of muslin with right sides facing and the edges aligned and pin them together along the sides. Sew (by hand or by machine) along the perimeter of the square with a ⅝" (16 mm) seam allowance. Leave a 7" (18 cm) opening on one side. Turn the fabric right-side out through the opening and press the seams. Stuff the pillowcase with the pillow insert. Turn the edges of the opening in ⅝" (16 mm) and pin. Hand-stitch the opening closed with a blind stitch *(Fig. 2)*.

The entire pillow can be hand-washed (or machine-washed on a delicate cycle) and air dried.

Fig. 1: Straight stitch (or Running Stitch)   *Fig. 2: Blind stitch*

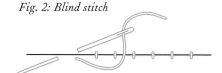

COILED BOWLS

WITH ERIN CONSIDINE

Erin's first fiber arts course in college led her to the ancient basketry technique of coiling, in which fibers are wound around each other in concentric rings. The textbook Erin learned from explained the process using jute, but she also experimented with rope, yarn, and wire, creating sculptural pieces in a variety of textures. For this project, Erin wrapped nylon clothesline cord with environmentally friendly hemp twine, which is available in natural tones as well as a rainbow of dyed colors. Hemp twine is tightly woven and extremely strong, and when used for coiling it results in compact, tidy bowls. The hemp is rough, so be aware that your fingers might get a little raw while wrapping. Using nylon cord as a core makes it easier to slide the hemp along the rope, plus it makes the repetitive coiling motions smoother. You may also want to adjust your hand movements slightly as you work to keep the twine from continuously rubbing the same area. If you wish to experiment with softer materials, try wrapping the coils with yarn, which will yield less rigid, fuzzier bowls. When picking your clothesline, remember that a thicker cord will make a thicker coil, and it will also build volume faster than a thinner cord. (Most hardware stores sell nylon clothesline cord by the foot in case you want to experiment with a few different gauges.) These bowls take patience and time, but the beautiful, heirloom-quality results are well worth the effort.

MATERIALS:

Nylon clothesline cord,
approximately 25' (8 m)

Hemp twine, one or several colors
(approximately 50' / 15 m needed for
a 5"/12.5-cm-wide bowl)

Tapestry needle

Scissors

Masking tape

Bottle, bowl, or pot to use as a form
(optional)

A) Tapered end

B) Wrap twine toward tapered end

C) Bend into a loop

G) Bring new twine up between coils

H) Secure new twine

I) Wrap tail of old twine under new twine

1. MAKE BASE OF BOWL: Snip one end of the cord with scissors to create a tapered end *(A)*. Cut a piece of twine 6' (1.8 m) long. Fold the twine in half and thread the ends through the tapestry needle. Don't knot the ends of the twine; simply pull the ends approximately 6" (15 cm) past the eye of the needle to create a long tail.

Hold the looped end of the twine flat against the cord, about 1" (2.5 cm) from the end of the cord, and wrap the doubled twine on the needle around the cord and through the loop, pulling tightly. Continue wrapping in the direction of the cut end of the cord *(B)*.

Pinch the end of the cord into a bent loop and hold it in place *(C)*. Wrap the twine around both pieces of cord in the loop until the loop is covered *(D)*. This will be the bottom-center of the bowl. Continue wrapping the twine around the cord for approximately 1" (2.5 cm), then coil the cord around the center of the bowl *(E)*. Wrap a loop around the outermost cord and then around the center of the coil, creating a figure-eight stitch that locks the 2 coils together *(F)*.

Wrap the twine 3 times around the outer cord and then wrap a figure eight to anchor the twine to the inner cord next to it. This is the pattern you will continue for the rest of the bowl: 3 winds of twine to cover the cord, a figure eight to anchor it, 3 winds of twine, a figure eight to anchor it, and so on.

D) Wrap loop with twine

E) Coil cord around center

F) Figure-eight locks coils together

J) Secure with figure eight

K) Start creating walls

L) Taper cord and finish

2. ADD TWINE: When you want to add more twine or change to a new color, stop with about 2" (5 cm) of the original twine remaining. Remove the needle, and thread another doubled 6' (1.8 m) length of twine onto the needle. Bring the threaded needle up between the coils, 2 coils away from where you will begin your next wrap *(G)*. Pull the needle through the loop to secure the new piece of twine to the coil *(H)*. Continue wrapping the twine around the coils as you did in Step 1, in figure-eight fashion, making sure to wrap the tail of the old twine under the new twine *(I + J)*.

3. MAKE SIDES AND FINISH: Once the base of your bowl is the desired diameter, start creating the walls by positioning the new section of nylon cord slightly above the previous coil *(K)*. You can do this "free form," manipulating the curve of the bowl as you go, or place a bottle, bowl, or pot on top of the coils and use the shape as a guide.

When the bowl is the desired size, snip the end of the cord with scissors to taper it *(L)*. Securely attach the last row to the previous row with figure eights, and then wrap the twine around the end of the cord and the previous row as if they were a single row. Thread the twine back through the figure eights, knot the end, and trim the excess twine.

WOVEN CAMERA STRAP

WITH ERIN CONSIDINE

I was introduced to Erin through a network of mutual friends while we were organizing and hosting sales for independent designers in Brooklyn. By the time I met Erin, she was already an experienced weaver—she had found a frame loom on the street in 2007 and started incorporating weaving into her metalsmith work.

Erin loves the relaxing, methodical nature of the weaving process and the gratifying feeling of creating a new textile. The type of weaving used for this project—called backstrap weaving—has its roots in ancient civilizations and utilizes a simple, portable loom. The yarn threads are stretched between the waist of the weaver and a stationary object (such as a doorknob or a hook). A backstrap loom kit can be purchased, but this project uses a loom made from scratch using chipboard (solid, dense cardboard). This homemade loom is perfect for creating a narrow strap that can be easily transformed into a camera strap when a metal swivel hook and key ring are sewn to either end.

MATERIALS:

White paper

Pencil

Scissors

All-purpose glue

Cutting mat

Utility knife or sharp heavy-duty box cutter

12" (30-cm)-square piece of chipboard

Awl

3 skeins sport-weight linen yarn,
in colors of your choice

Micro latch hook or embroidery needle

Stainless steel ruler

Set of joined chopsticks (ideally chopsticks
that are rounded rather than rectangular)

Bulldog clip

4' (1.2 m) scrap yarn (slightly thicker than
the linen yarn)

Two 2" (5 cm) metal swivel hooks

Two 1/2" to 1" (12 mm to 2.5 cm) metal
key rings

WEAVING PARTS AND TERMS *(Fig. 1)*

WARP: set of yarns that are parallel to the selvedge, or the longer dimension of a woven construction.

WEFT: set of yarns that are perpendicular to the selvedge, or the width of a woven construction.

BEATER/BATTEN: thin strip of chipboard used to pack the weft into position.

HEDDLE: chipboard structure through which the warp threads are passed.

SELVEDGE: lengthwise (or warp-wise) edge of a woven fabric; the point at which the weft yarns turn and bind the warp to form a finished edge.

SHUTTLE: chipboard structures wound with yarn used to carry the weft strands back and forth between the warp strands.

SHED: space between separated warp yarns through which the shuttle (wrapped with weft yarn) is passed. Raising or lowering the heddle creates a shed.

Fig. 1: Assembled Loom Parts

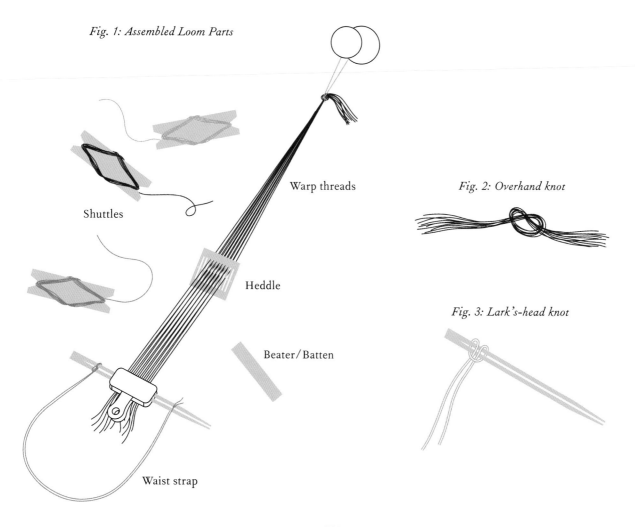

Warp threads

Shuttles

Heddle

Beater/Batten

Waist strap

Fig. 2: Overhand knot

Fig. 3: Lark's-head knot

A) Insert warp strands
through holes

B) Insert warp strands through slots

C) Rake warp strands to
neaten them

1. SET UP: You will need a doorknob or hook on which to hang your loom and approximately 6' (1.8 m) of space in front of the doorknob or hook to extend the loom. A simple cup hook from the hardware store, securely attached to your wall, will work well. You can weave standing up, sitting on the floor, or sitting in a chair. The doorknob or hook should be slightly above you as you weave. Experiment with what is most comfortable for you.

2. CONSTRUCT LOOM PARTS: Lay white paper on top of the heddle, shuttle, and beater/batten templates on page 166. Trace around the templates with a pencil, tracing the shuttle template 3 times, and use scissors to cut out the shapes. For the heddle, fold the cut-out paper in half, then cut out the negative spaces inside the long rectangles. These are your loom part templates.

Glue the templates onto the chipboard and let them dry thoroughly. Place the chipboard on the cutting mat. Using the ruler and utility knife, carefully cut out the shapes from the chipboard. Always cut away from your body, and make shallow cuts along the same line several times rather than trying to make one deep cut. Use the awl to puncture the holes in the heddle template, being careful not to get too close to the edges of the slots of the heddle.

3. MAKE WARP: For a 1¾" (4.5-cm) wide strap you will need fourteen 6' (1.8 m) pieces of yarn. The warp threads will not be visible in the weave, so any color yarn can be used. Cut the yarn and knot one end with an overhand knot *(Fig. 2)*. Trim the other end of the yarn strands to make them even. To thread (or "load") the warp strands through the heddle, you will thread each strand individually onto a needle and insert it through a hole *(A)* or a slot *(B)* in the heddle. Note that for the camera strap shown on page 153, you will only need 14 warp strands. When loading a heddle with fewer strands than there are holes/slots, start from the middle and work your way out, so that the strands are centered on the heddle rather than to one side. Begin by threading half the warp strands through the holes in the heddle. Then, thread the remaining half of the strands through the long rectangular slots in the heddle. When all of the strands are through the heddle, gently rake them out with your fingers to organize the strands *(C)*. The heddle should be positioned about halfway down the length of the warp strands.

4. ASSEMBLE LOOM PARTS:

LOAD SHUTTLES: Take a ball of yarn and hold the tail of the yarn to one of the flat sides of a shuttle. Wrap the yarn around the sides of the shuttle in a figure-eight pattern *(D)*. Don't overload the shuttle—a ¼" (6 mm) bulge around the cardboard is best. Make a shuttle for each color of yarn.

MAKE WAIST STRAP: Cut 6' (1.8 m) of yarn, any color, and fold it in half. With the folded end, make a lark's-head knot *(Fig. 3)*, insert the chopsticks into the loop, and pull the knot tight. To keep the knot from slipping, weave the tails between the legs of the chopsticks. Place the chopsticks at approximately belly-button level (or lower if that's more comfortable for you) and about 4" (10 cm) away from your torso. Wrap the yarn around your body and make an overhand knot with the tail ends of the yarn to loop over the open end of the chopsticks. Undo the waist strap and set it aside.

ASSEMBLE LOOM: To attach the warp strands to the doorknob or hook, cut 2' (60 cm) of scrap yarn. Fold the yarn in half and make a lark's-head knot around the knotted end of the warp threads. Knot the end of the scrap yarn with an overhand knot and attach it to the doorknob or hook.

To attach the warp strands to the waist strap, separate the warp strands into 4 approximately equal sections and tie each section to the chopsticks with an overhand knot *(E)*. Roll the chopsticks several times toward the wall *(F)* and secure the strands to the chopsticks with the bulldog clip. Wrap the waist strap around your waist and secure the strap to the open end of the chopsticks *(G)*. *Fig. 1* shows what an assembled warp/heddle/waist strap contraption looks like.

Note: If a hole in the heddle breaks open, it can be fixed by wrapping the column of the heddle with tape and punching a hole through it with the awl. The loose warp thread can be untied from the doorknob and threaded back through the heddle.

5. WEAVE WITH SCRAP YARN: The basic weaving process is done by lifting and lowering the heddle and passing the weft yarn back and forth from side to side. When you raise or lower the heddle and lean back (creating some tension in the warp), all of the warp yarns that are threaded through the holes will separate from the yarns that are threaded through the rectangular slots. The space between these two rows of warp yarns is called the shed. In order to weave, you will lift the heddle to create one position of the shed and pass the yarn through to the other side *(Fig. 4A)*, and then lower the heddle to create the second position of the shed and pass the weft yarn back through *(Fig. 4B)* (the warp is shown in two colors here to clarify the strands, but when weaving, you will only use one color). The beater/batten is inserted into the shed and pulled down onto the weaving to compact it after each change in the shed.

Before beginning with the strap yarn, the warp threads need to be evened out by weaving with scrap yarn. (The scrap yarn will be removed later and you won't see it in the finished weaving.) Cut a piece of scrap yarn approximately 2' (60 cm) and bundle it in a figure eight between your index finger and thumb (when using a small amount of yarn, a shuttle isn't necessary).

Start with the scrap yarn on the right side of the warp. Lift the heddle and pass the scrap yarn bundle through to the left side of the warp. Pull the heddle down and beat the yarn in. Pass the bundle back to the right side *(H)*. Repeat for approximately 10 rows, until the warp threads are evenly spaced *(I)*. Beat in the yarn with each row. When the warp threads are evenly spaced, cut the scrap yarn.

D) Loading a shuttle

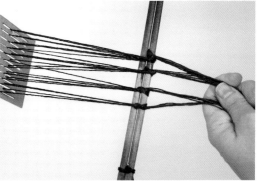

E) Tie warp strands to chopsticks

F) Roll chopsticks toward wall

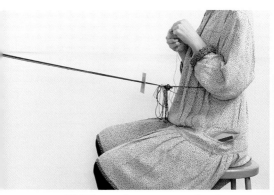

G) Wrap waist strap around waist

H) Start weaving with scrap yarn

I) Continue with scrap yarn until warp is evenly spaced

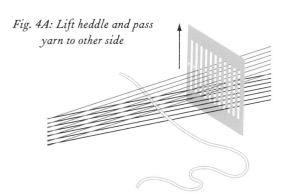

Fig. 4A: Lift heddle and pass yarn to other side

Fig. 4B: Lower heddle and pass yarn back

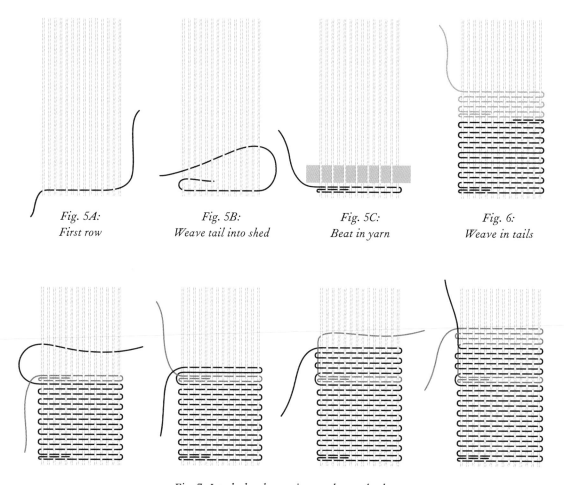

Fig. 5A:
First row

Fig. 5B:
Weave tail into shed

Fig. 5C:
Beat in yarn

Fig. 6:
Weave in tails

Fig. 7: Interlock color not in use along selvedge

6. WEAVE STRAP (WEFT): Decide on the first color you want to use for your strap. Open the shed, pass the shuttle from left to right, and beat the yarn in, leaving a ¾" (19 mm) tail *(Fig. 5A; J + K)*. Change the shed position and pass the shuttle back from right to left; at the same time, weave the tail into the shed *(Fig. 5B)*. To keep the edges even and straight, it's best to pass the yarn through loosely, holding the weft thread to the outermost warp thread, setting the weft yarn at an angle (about 45 degrees), and then beating it in to even out the yarn *(Fig. 5C; L + M)*. For this project we created a tightly beaten strap that is strong and somewhat stiff. Utilize your body weight to maintain a consistent tension in the warp threads throughout the entire weaving process. This prevents the woven strap from drawing inward and tugging, which creates uneven edges. Continue weaving until you would like to switch colors or you run out of weft yarn.

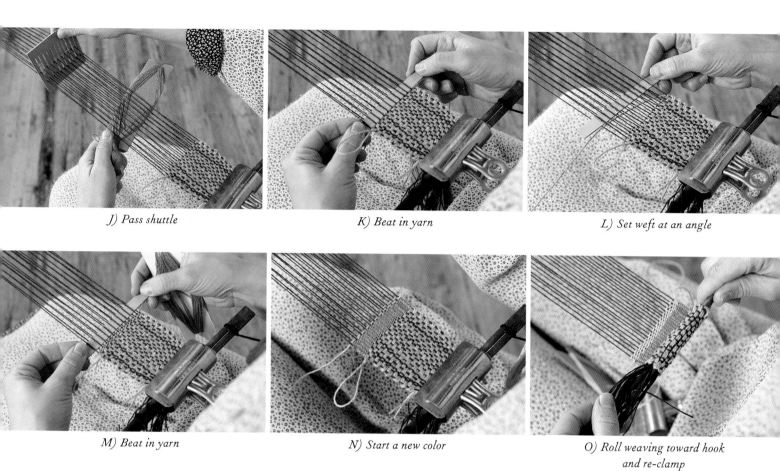

J) Pass shuttle

K) Beat in yarn

L) Set weft at an angle

M) Beat in yarn

N) Start a new color

O) Roll weaving toward hook
and re-clamp

7. CHANGE WEFT YARNS: When you would like to add a new color or the weft yarn runs out, you will need to weave in the tail of the finished yarn and the tail of the new yarn, similarly to how you the weaved the tail in at the beginning of a strand *(Fig. 6; N)*.

For this project, new colors are used in two ways: The first is to gradually alternate colors by weaving one row (right to left) with one color, and a second row (left to right) with a second color. This technique will create a 1x1 color change in a single row (e.g., purple, yellow, purple, yellow, etc.). The second technique is to create a solid-colored stripe with a new color by working back and forth (right to left, then left to right) in a single color.

If you are making 1x1 color changes in a single row or solid single-row stripes, you can leave both shuttles attached rather than ending and beginning a new yarn each time. To do this, you will need to run the color not in use along the selvedge, interlocking it as you weave with the other color of weft yarn *(Fig. 7)*.

8. ADJUST YOUR POSITION: As your weaving grows, you'll end up scooting farther and farther away from the wall in order to maintain proper tension. Every 12" (30 cm) or so, undo your waist strap and slide the weaving between the legs of the chopsticks, roll it toward the hook or doorknob *(O)*, and clamp it again with the clip.

COLOR PATTERN FOR PURPLE (P)/CORAL (C)/YELLOW (Y) STRAP (Repeat entire pattern twice)

P 50 rows	Y 1 row	Y 16 rows
C 1 row	C 16 rows	P 2 rows
P 16 rows	Y 2 rows	Y 12 rows
C 2 rows	C 12 rows	P 2 rows
P 12 rows	Y 2 rows	Y 3 rows
C 2 rows	C 3 rows	P 2 rows
P 3 rows	Y 2 rows	Y 3 rows
C 2 rows	C 3 rows	P 1 row ⎫
P 3 rows	Y 1 row ⎫	Y 1 row ⎭ repeat 15 times
C 1 row ⎫	C 1 row ⎭ repeat 15 times	P 6 rows
P 1 row ⎭ repeat 15 times	Y 6 rows	Y 2 rows
C 6 rows	C 2 rows	P 8 rows
P 2 rows	Y 8 rows	Y 2 rows
C 8 rows	C 2 rows	P 13 rows
P 2 rows	Y 13 rows	Y 1 row
C 13 rows	C 1 row	P 50 rows
P 1 row	Y 50 rows	
C 50 rows	P 1 row	

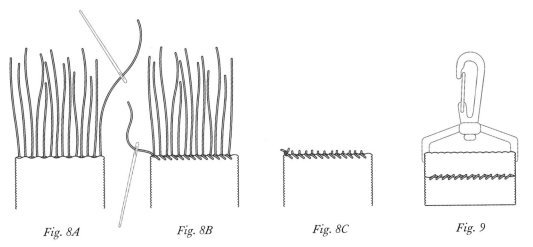

Fig. 8A   *Fig. 8B*   *Fig. 8C*   *Fig. 9*

9. FINISH STRAP: When you have finished weaving, unhook and untie both ends of the strap. Remove the heddle and leave the warp threads long *(Fig. 8A)*. Untangle the threads with your fingers and remove the scrap yarn. Using one of the outer warp threads, sew into the weft threads using a whipstitch *(Fig. 8B)*. Trim the excess threads *(Fig. 8C)*.

Fold one end of the strap around a swivel hook and sew it in place with an overcast or hemming stitch *(Fig. 9)*. Repeat with the other side. If the swivel hook is too big to hook onto your camera, attach key rings.

TEMPLATES

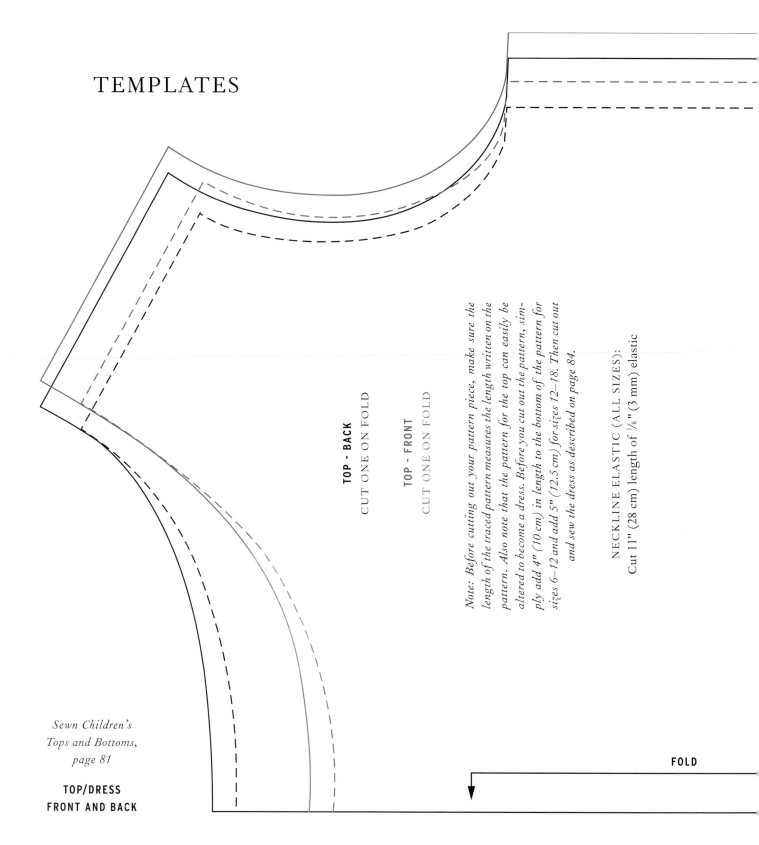

TOP - BACK

CUT ONE ON FOLD

TOP - FRONT

CUT ONE ON FOLD

Note: Before cutting out your pattern piece, make sure the length of the traced pattern measures the length written on the pattern. Also note that the pattern for the top can easily be altered to become a dress. Before you cut out the pattern, simply add 4" (10 cm) in length to the bottom of the pattern for sizes 6–12 and add 5" (12.5 cm) for sizes 12–18. Then cut out and sew the dress as described on page 84.

NECKLINE ELASTIC (ALL SIZES):
Cut 11" (28 cm) length of ⅛" (3 mm) elastic

Sewn Children's Tops and Bottoms, page 81

TOP/DRESS FRONT AND BACK

FOLD

162

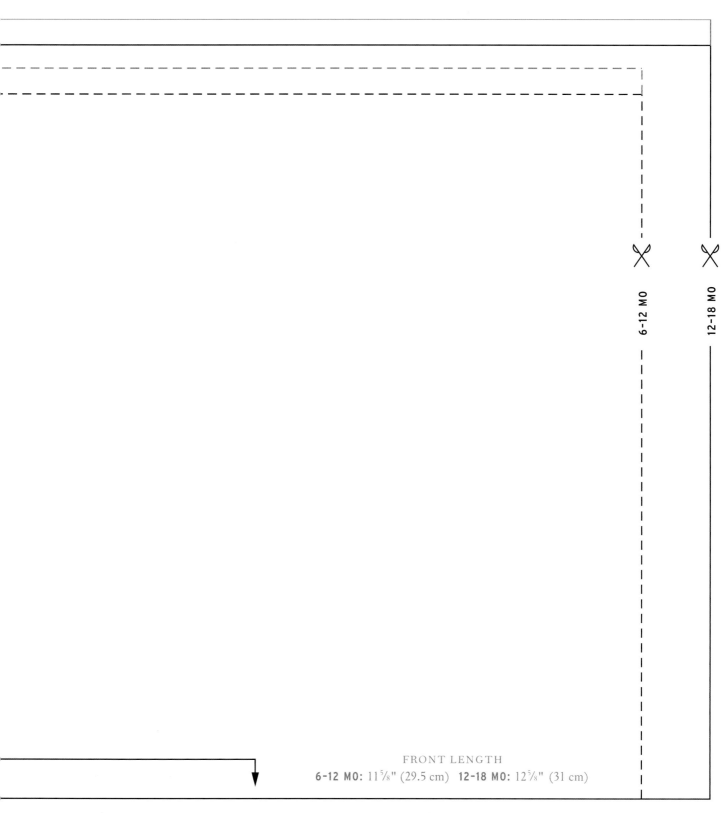

FRONT LENGTH
6-12 MO: 11⅝" (29.5 cm) **12-18 MO:** 12⅝" (31 cm)

6-12 MO

12-18 MO

BACK LENGTH
6-12 MO: 12¾" (33 cm) **12-18 MO:** 13¾" (35 cm)

PANTS/BLOOMERS

BLOOMER LENGTH
6-12 MO: 10½" (26.5 cm)   **12-18 MO:** 11⅝" (29.5 cm)

PANT LENGTH
6-12 MO: 15⅜" (39 cm)   **12-18 MO:** 16½" (42 cm)

6-12 MO: cut 15½" (39.5 cm) length of ½" (12 mm) elastic
12-18 MO: cut 16½" (42 cm) length of ½" (12 mm) elastic

PANTS/BLOOMERS - FRONT/BACK
CUT TWO ON FOLD

Note: Before cutting out your pattern piece, make sure the length of the traced pattern measures the length written on the pattern.

FOLD

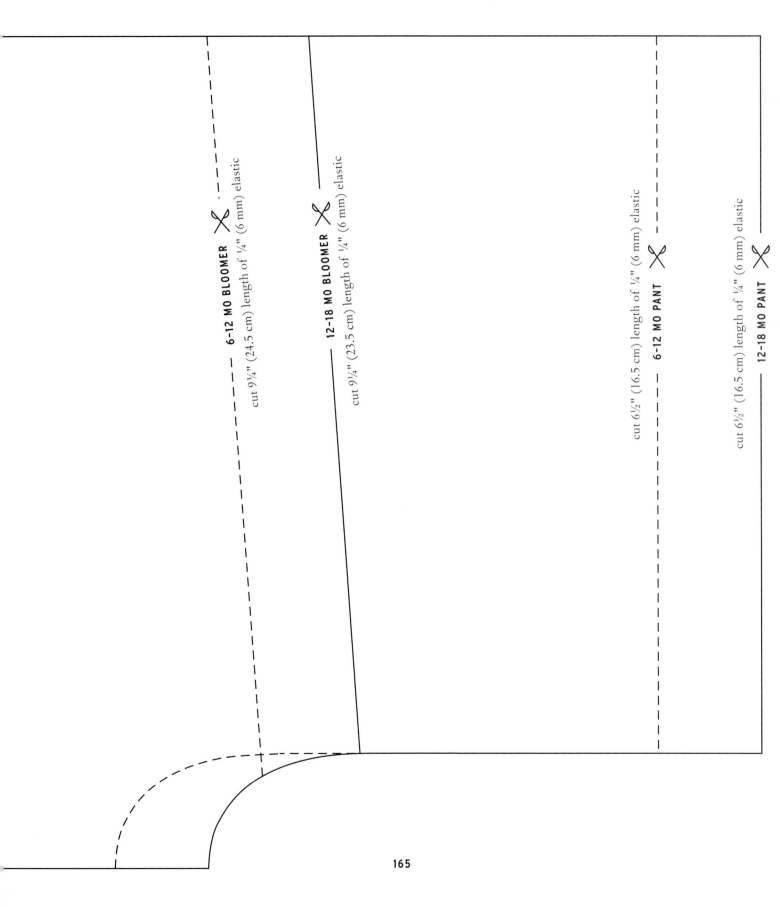

6-12 MO BLOOMER ✂

cut 9¾" (24.5 cm) length of ¼" (6 mm) elastic

12-18 MO BLOOMER ✂

cut 9¼" (23.5 cm) length of ¼" (6 mm) elastic

cut 6½" (16.5 cm) length of ¼" (6 mm) elastic

6-12 MO PANT ✂

cut 6½" (16.5 cm) length of ¼" (6 mm) elastic

12-18 MO PANT ✂

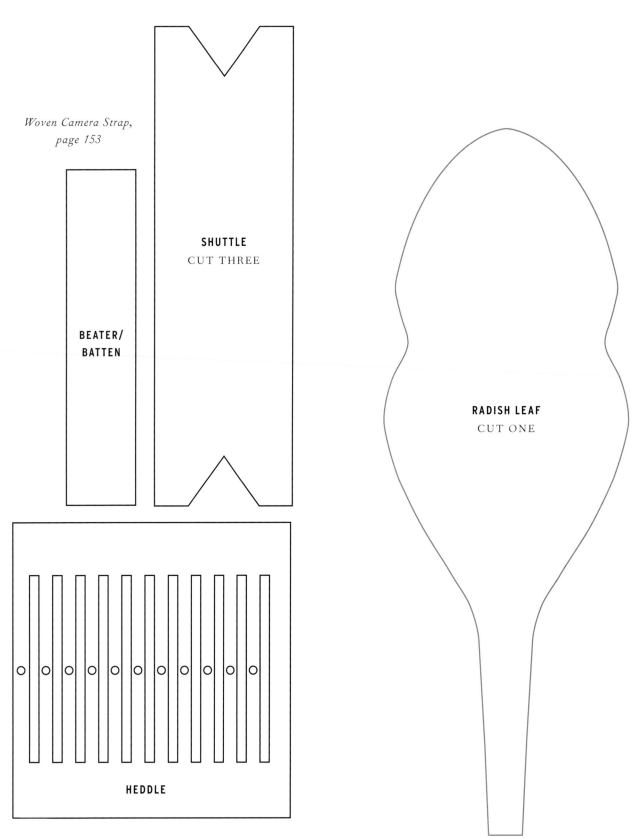

Woven Camera Strap,
page 153

SHUTTLE
CUT THREE

BEATER/
BATTEN

RADISH LEAF
CUT ONE

HEDDLE

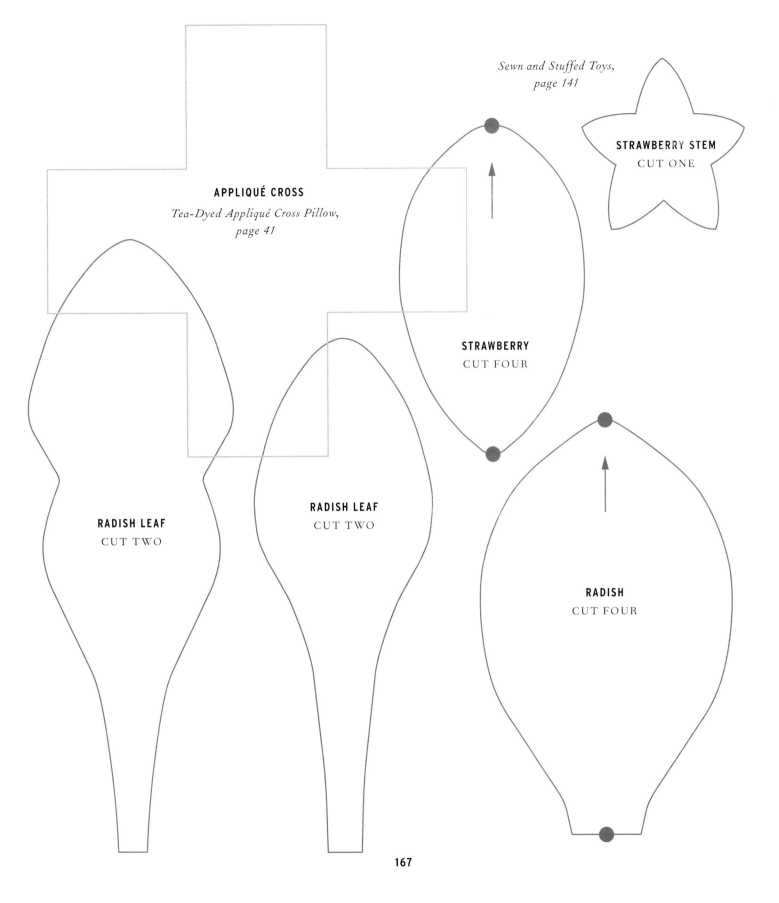

APPLIQUÉ CROSS
Tea-Dyed Appliqué Cross Pillow, page 41

Sewn and Stuffed Toys, page 141

STRAWBERRY STEM
CUT ONE

STRAWBERRY
CUT FOUR

RADISH LEAF
CUT TWO

RADISH LEAF
CUT TWO

RADISH
CUT FOUR

SPECIAL TECHNIQUES

MACHINE-SEWING BASICS

Before you cut out your fabric and start sewing, you will want to wash and dry the fabric in the same way that you will wash and dry the garment once it is finished (check the manufacturer's instructions to be safe). Doing this will preshrink the fabric, so there will be minimal shrinkage once the completed garment is later washed. Iron the fabric after it has been dried so it will be free of wrinkles.

For the sewing projects included in this book, you will need a sewing machine, thread in a color that matches your fabric, an iron and ironing board, both fabric and paper scissors, straight pins, and a disappearing-ink fabric pen or tailor's chalk for tracing around patterns. All other specific tools will be mentioned in the materials list at the beginning of the project.

TRACING AND CUTTING OUT PATTERNS

All woven fabrics have *SELVEDGES* (narrow borders on either side that keep the edges of the fabric from unraveling). The woven fabric itself is usually composed of warp and weft threads that cross each other at a 90-degree

Fig. 1: Cutting fabric on the fold

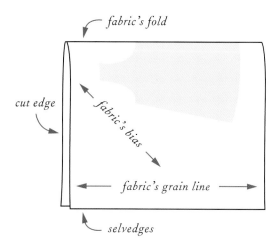

- fabric's fold

cut edge

fabric's bias

fabric's grain line

- selvedges

angle; the threads that run in the same direction as the selvedge constitute the fabric's *GRAIN LINE*. When a pattern instructs you to cut out a pattern piece along the grain line, it means that the arrow marked "grain line" on the pattern piece should run in the same direction as the threads that run parallel to the selvedge. In cases where a pattern is to be cut out "on the fold," you should always fold your fabric selvedge to selvedge and place the "fold" edge of the pattern piece on the fabric's folded edge *(Fig. 1)*.

In order to use the pattern pieces in this book, simply lay a piece of tracing paper or white paper over the pattern pieces and trace around them. If the pattern stretches across the entire spread of the book, make sure to wedge the tracing paper into the center crease of the book in order to trace the entire pattern, and then check that the length of your traced pattern is the same length as the measurement written in the instructions. Make sure to also copy over any information from the pattern, such as fold lines, notches, or quantities to cut, onto your cut paper pattern. Cut out the pattern pieces with paper scissors. You can either pin the pattern pieces to the fabric or trace around the pattern pieces with a disappearing-ink fabric pen or tailor's chalk; then cut out the pattern pieces with fabric scissors.

When a pattern refers to a *WRONG SIDE* or a *RIGHT SIDE* of the fabric, it is referring to the side that you would typically see on the outside of the garment (the right side) or the side that is usually on the inside (the wrong side).

SEWING BASICS

Before you start sewing, check your sewing machine's manual to learn how to set it up. Most important, make sure you have threaded your machine properly—you will need a spool of thread for the top of your machine, which will feed down to the needle, as well as a threaded bobbin.

For all of the projects in this book, you can use a *STRAIGHT STITCH* with a medium stitch length. Before you start sewing, sew a few rows onto scraps of your project fabric to make sure you are happy with the stitch tension. If the stitches are too loose or too tight, adjust the tension settings on the machine until the stitches look nice and even on both sides of the fabric.

BACKTACKING secures the stitches at the beginning or end of a row, ensuring that they won't unravel later. To backtack at the beginning of a stitch line, simply lower the needle into the fabric a few stitches ahead of where you want to begin and sew in reverse for a few stitches, then continue sewing forward. To backtack at the end of a stitch line, simply sew in reverse for a few stitches before breaking the thread.

An *EDGE STITCH* is essentially a straight stitch that is sewn very close to the folded or sewn edge of the fabric. In order to make your edge stitches nice and even, you might find it helpful to take off the standard presser foot on your machine and temporarily replace it with an edge-stitch foot.

KNITTING BASICS

CASTING ON

In this book, we recommend using a technique called a Long-Tail Cast-On. Your cast-on row will create your very first row of stitches in your knitted fabric.

1. Pull out a length of yarn from your skein that is about four times longer than the length you'll be casting on. At the midpoint of this length, make a slipknot and place it onto one of the needles *(Fig. 1A–1C)*. The slipknot is technically your first stitch.

2. Hold the needle in your right hand and wrap one tail of the yarn around your left index finger, and the other tail of yarn around your thumb *(Fig. 1D)*.

3. Use your needle tip to pick up the yarn in front of your thumb; slip the needle underneath the yarn on your index finger; then bring the needle with the yarn from your index finger down through the loop on your thumb *(Fig. 1E)*.

CASTING ON

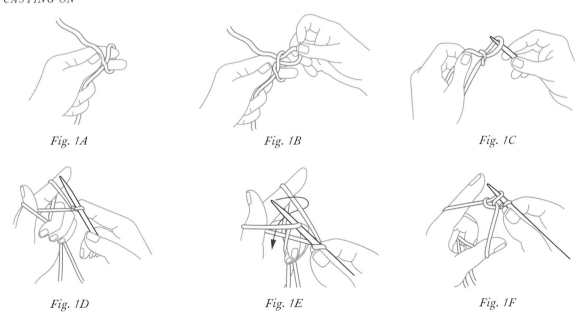

Fig. 1A

Fig. 1B

Fig. 1C

Fig. 1D

Fig. 1E

Fig. 1F

4. Remove your thumb from the loop, then insert your thumb under the strand coming from the loop, and gently pull the new loop so it sits snug (but not too snug) on the needle *(Fig. 1F)*. The yarn should now be back in the original position. Repeat until you have the desired number of stitches on the needle.

KNIT STITCH

1. To make a knit stitch, hold the needle with the stitches in your left hand. Hold the yarn to the back of your work and insert the tip of the right-hand needle up underneath the front "leg" of the first stitch on the needle *(Fig. 2A)*.

2. Pick up the yarn in the back and wrap it around the tip of the right-hand needle in a counter-clockwise direction *(Fig. 2B)*.

3. Use your right-hand needle tip to bring the yarn through the stitch to the front of the work *(Fig. 2C)*.

4. With the new stitch securely on the right-hand needle, gently pull the old stitch to the right, so it comes off the left-hand needle *(Fig. 2D)*. Repeat with every stitch on the left-hand needle to work a row of knit stitches.

PURL STITCH

1. To make a purl stitch, hold needle with the stitches in your left hand. Bring the yarn to the front of your work between the needles and insert the tip of the right-hand needle under the front "leg" of the first stitch, from back to front *(Fig. 3A)*.

2. Pick up the yarn in the front and wrap it around the tip of the right-hand needle in a counter-clockwise direction *(Fig. 3B)*.

3. Use your right-hand needle tip to bring the yarn back through the stitch *(Fig. 3C)*.

4. With the new stitch securely on the right-hand needle, gently pull the old stitch to the right, so it comes off the left-hand needle *(Fig. 3D)*. Repeat with every stitch on the left-hand needle to work a row of purl stitches.

SPECIAL STITCHES

Once you have mastered the knit stitch and the purl stitch, you can use them in combination to create interesting textures and to shape your knitting.

KNIT STITCH

Fig. 2A

Fig. 2B

Fig. 2C

Fig. 2D

PURL STITCH

Fig. 3A

Fig. 3B

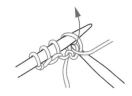

Fig. 3C

Fig. 3D

STOCKINETTE STITCH: This is the most common stitch combination, creating a smooth "right side" of the fabric and a bumpy "wrong side" of the fabric. If you are working in the round, simply knit all stitches. If you are working back and forth to create a flat piece of fabric, alternate one row of knit stitches with one row of purl stitches.

GARTER STITCH: This combination of stitches creates a nubby, ridged fabric that is the same on both sides. If you are working in the round, alternate one round of knit stitches with one round of purl stitches. If you are working back and forth to create a flat piece of fabric, simply knit all rows.

INCREASING: In order to make a piece of knitted fabric wider, the instructions will sometimes tell you to knit into the front and back of a stitch, which will add one stitch to your row. To do this, insert your needle into the stitch as if to knit and work the stitch as usual, but before you take the stitch off the left-hand needle, slide the right-hand needle under the back loop of the stitch. Wrap the yarn around the needle again *(Fig. 4A)*, as if knitting normally, and pull a new loop forward, then slip the original stitch and the new stitch off the left-hand needle. There will now be two stitches on your right-hand needle instead of one *(Fig. 4B)*.

DECREASING: In order to make a piece of knitted fabric narrower, you can work two stitches together (usually called "knit 2 together" or "k2tog"), which will decrease one stitch. To do this, slide your right-hand needle into the first two stitches on the left-hand needle as if to knit *(Fig. 5A)*. (It helps to go up through the leg of the second stitch first, and then through the leg of the fist stitch.) Knit the two stitches together as though they were one *(Fig. 5B)*.

Another way to decrease a stitch is to slip the first stitch on the left-hand needle as if to knit onto the right-hand needle, knit one stitch, and then pick up the slipped stitch with your left-hand needle tip and slip the stitch up and over the knitted stitch, dropping it off the needle (this is usually called "skp").

WORKING IN THE ROUND

In some cases, like with socks, you will want to knit in the round to create a tube of fabric. To do this, use double-pointed needles to knit in the round.

1. To use double-pointed needles, cast all of your stitches onto one needle, then divide the stitches evenly among three or four needles (depending on what the pattern tells you to do). Make sure that all of your stitches are facing the same direction (there should be "knots" on one side and "loops" on the other side).

2. When you are positive that the stitches are not twisted, arrange the needles so that the needle with the ball of yarn coming from it is on the right, and the first stitch you're going to work is on the left-hand needle. Slip the tip of a free needle into the first stitch on the left-hand needle, and use the yarn from the right-hand needle to make a stitch. This will connect your work into a loop *(Fig. 6)*.

INCREASING

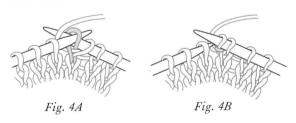

Fig. 4A   Fig. 4B

DECREASING

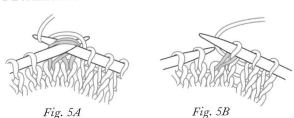

Fig. 5A   Fig. 5B

WORKING IN THE ROUND

Fig. 6

3. Continue knitting across all of the stitches on the first needle, and when you reach the end, the needle that was holding the stitches will become "free." Use that newly freed needle to continue knitting across the next needle.

4. Continue all the way around until you reach the beginning, where you first joined the work. Place a stitch marker here so you'll always know where your round begins.

(Note: If, after a few rounds of knitting, you see that there is a twist in your work, you have to rip it all out and start over.)

WORKING BACK AND FORTH

When you are knitting a flat piece of fabric (like a scarf or a blanket), you will most likely be working back and forth in rows. To do this, simply work all of the stitches on the left-hand needle, and when you run out of stitches, turn your work around so that the other side of the fabric is facing you (all of the stitches should once again be on your left-hand needle). Beginning with the first loop on the needle, start working the next row. Remember that if you are creating knit stitches, hold your yarn to the back, and if you are creating purl stitches, hold your yarn to the front.

BINDING OFF (both knitwise and purlwise)

When you are finished knitting, you need to bind off your stitches. This is how you get your work off the needles and secure the last row of stitches, which keeps your work from unraveling.

1. To bind off, knit the first two stitches in the row. Slip the point of the left-hand needle through the right-most stitch on the right-hand needle *(Fig. 7A)*, and lift it up and over the second stitch, dropping it off the needle *(Fig. 7B)*. One stitch will remain on the right-hand needle *(Fig. 7C)*.

2. Knit another stitch from the left-hand needle and repeat Step 1, lifting the right-most stitch up, over, and off the needle.

3. Continue to work stitches this way until you have only one stitch left on your needle. Cut the yarn, leaving a long tail. Bring the tail through the remaining stitch and tug it closed.

SEWING UP

To sew two pieces of knitting together, do so by placing the pieces to be joined side by side on a flat surface, with the right sides facing up. Thread a tapestry needle with a length of yarn and pull the fabric apart so you can see "ladders," or horizontal bars, between the stitches. Starting at a bottom corner, bring the needle underneath two of these ladders. Working vertically, bring the needle over to the opposite piece of fabric, and slide the needle beneath two ladders there. Go back to the first piece and

BINDING OFF

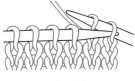

Fig. 7A *Fig. 7B*

Fig. 7C

SEWING UP

Fig. 8

PICKING UP AND KNITTING STITCHES

Fig. 9

keep sewing this way. You will see your stitches form a ladder along the seam. Pull tight every few stitches to close up the seam *(Fig. 8)*.

PICKING UP AND KNITTING STITCHES

To pick up and knit new stitches along the top or side edge of a piece of knitting, you can either use your knitting needles or a crochet hook. To do this, have the right side of the knitting facing you and begin on the right-hand side of the knitting. Slide your needle or hook into the edge of the knitting, going under both strands of yarn. Wrap the yarn around the needle or hook (as if to knit) and pull the yarn forward to the front of the knitting *(Fig. 9)*. Repeat for every stitch or row of stitches on the knitting. If you're using a crochet hook to pick up stitches, you'll need to transfer the stitches onto a knitting needle once you're done (or at intervals as you go). Once you have picked up all of the stitches, continue knitting normally.

CROCHET BASICS

All of the crochet patterns in this book are worked in the round, beginning with a slipknot (see *Figs. 1A - 1C* on page 169). The slipknot should be loose enough to slide along the hook, but not so loose as to slip off entirely.

YARN OVER AND CHAIN

All crochet stitches are created with different combinations of a basic yarn-over hooking action. To practice the hooking action and create a chain, insert your hook into the slipknot. Hold the slipknot between the thumb and

ring finger of your left hand and bring the yarn over the index finger of your left hand to create tension. With your right hand, hook the yarn as shown *(Fig. 1)* (also called a "yarn over"), and pull it through the slipknot on the hook. To create a chain, simply repeat this hooking action.

WORKING ROUNDS

To work in the round, you will begin with a center ring of stitches and work outward in circles. Most frequently, a center ring is comprised of several chain stitches joined together with a slip stitch. To work a slip stitch, slide the hook into the center loop of the indicated stitch, yarn over, and draw the hook back through the stitch AND through the loop that was originally on the hook, joining the two together *(Figs. 2A + 2B)*.

When working rounds, the stitches can either be worked into the center of the ring, or into each chain stitch.

CROCHET STITCHES

All of these stitches can be worked in the round, and unless the instructions state otherwise, assume that all stitches are worked beneath the two strands of yarn at the top of the next stitch (or front of the chain).

SINGLE CROCHET (sc)

Single crochet starts much like a slip stitch.

1. Slip the hook into the center of the indicated stitch. Yarn over, and draw the hook back through the first loop on the hook *(Fig. 3A)*.

2. Yarn over again, and draw the hook through the two remaining loops *(Fig. 3B)*.

YARN OVER

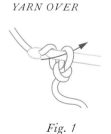

Fig. 1

WORKING ROUNDS

Fig. 2A

Fig. 2B

SINGLE CROCHET

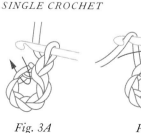

Fig. 3A

Fig. 3B

173

HALF-DOUBLE CROCHET (hdc)

1. Yarn over the hook, and insert it into the center of the indicated stitch.

2. Yarn over again, drawing the wrapped hook back through the same stitch. You should now have three loops on the hook.

3. Yarn over a third time, and draw the hook through all three loops at once *(Fig. 4A)*, finishing the stitch in one step *(Fig. 4B)*.

DOUBLE CROCHET (dc)

Double crochet is an expanded form of half double crochet.

1. Yarn over the hook, and insert it into the center of the indicated stitch. Yarn over the hook again, drawing the wrapped hook back through the same stitch. You should now have three loops on the hook.

2. Now, instead of drawing the hook through all three loops as in a half double crochet, yarn over, and pull the hook through the first two loops only (there should now be two loops remaining) *(Fig. 5A)*.

3. Yarn over, drawing the hook through the remaining two loops on the hook *(Fig. 5B)* to finish the stitch *(Fig. 5C)*.

TREBLE CROCHET (tr)

1. Yarn over the hook two times and insert it into the center of the indicated stitch. Yarn over the hook again, drawing the wrapped hook through the same stitch. You should now have four loops on the hook.

2. Yarn over and pull the hook through the first two loops on the hook *(Fig. 6A)*.

3. Yarn over and pull the hook through two more loops *(Fig. 6B)*.

4. Yarn over once more, drawing the hook through the remaining two loops on the hook *(Fig. 6C)* to finish the stitch *(Fig. 6D)*.

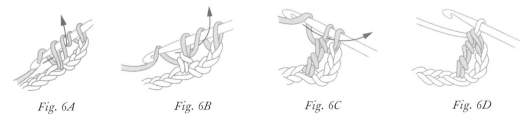

HALF DOUBLE CROCHET

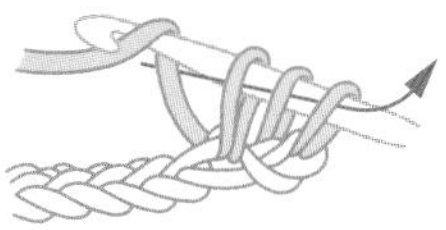

Fig. 4A 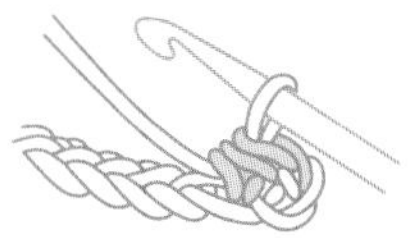   Fig. 4B

DOUBLE CROCHET

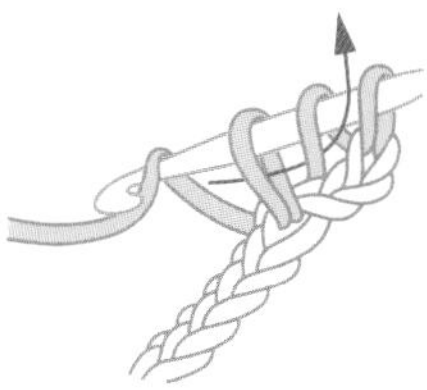

Fig. 5A 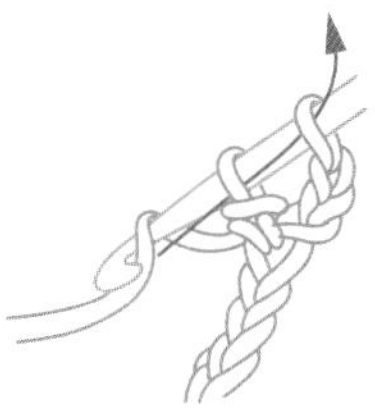   Fig. 5B    Fig. 5C

TREBLE CROCHET

Fig. 6A   Fig. 6B   Fig. 6C   Fig. 6D

RESOURCES

The materials and tools used in the projects in this book are generally available at art supply and craft stores nationwide. If you cannot find what you are looking for locally, try these online sources:

ART AND CRAFT SUPPLIES:

A.C. Moore *(acmoore.com)*

Dharma Trading Co. *(dharmatrading.com)*

Dick Blick Art Materials *(dickblick.com)*

Michaels Stores *(michaels.com)*

Pearl Paint *(pearlpaint.com)*

Utrecht Art Supplies *(utrechtart.com)*

CANDLE-MAKING SUPPLIES:

The Candlemaker *(thecandlemaker.com)*

eBeeHoney.com

JEWELRY-MAKING SUPPLIES:

Fire Mountain Gems and Beads *(firemountaingems.com)*

Metalliferous *(metalliferous.com)*

Toho Shoji *(tohoshoji-ny.com)*

KAPOK STUFFING AND BUCKWHEAT HULLS:

Carolina Morning Designs *(zafu.net/buckwheat)*

YARN, FABRIC, AND THREAD:

EnviroTextiles *(envirotextiles.com)*

Jo-Ann Fabrics and Craft Stores *(joann.com)*

Mood Fabrics *(moodfabrics.com)*

Purl Soho *(purlsoho.com)*

The majority of the fabric and yarn used in this book was provided by Purl Soho in New York City (purlsoho.com). For a list of specific materials used for each project, see below:

ROTARY-PRINTED CLOTH NAPKINS: *Robert Kaufman Essex, Yarn Dyed Cotton Fabric*

SCREEN-PRINTED MULTICOLOR FABRIC: *Robert Kaufman Organic, Canvas Deluxe Fabric*

SEWN DRESS AND TOP: *Kiyohara Linen-Cotton Blend Fabric*

KNITTED SOCKS: *Koigu Painter's Palette Premium Merino Yarn, Anzula Squishy Merino/Cashmere/Nylon Blend Yarn*

TEA-DYED APPLIQUÉ CROSS PILLOW: *Mary Flanagan Felted Wool Fabric, Robert Kaufman Organic Voile Fabric*

EMBROIDERY SAMPLER: *DMC Embroidery Floss, Londonderry Linen Thread, Zweigart Cross Stitch Linen Fabric*

FABRIC ORIGAMI: *Robert Kaufman Waterford Linen Fabric, DMC Metallic Embroidery Floss*

SEWN CHILDREN'S TOPS AND BOTTOMS: *Liberty of London Tana Lawn Classics Cotton Fabric, Kokka Fabrics Fine Solids Fabric*

WOVEN PLACEMATS: *Rowan Fabrics Shot Cotton Fabric, Liberty of London Tana Lawn Classics Cotton Fabric*

KNITTED CAT TOYS: *Madelinetosh Tosh Merino DK Yarn, Koigu Premium Merino Yarn*

FREEFORM KNITTED THROW: *Swans Island Worsted Yarn, Cascade Yarns Eco Highland Duo Yarn, Cascade Yarns Eco Cloud Yarn Anzula for Better or Worsted Yarn, Brooklyn Tweed Shelter Yarn, Blue Sky Worsted Hand Dyes Yarn*

CROCHETED GARLAND: *Louet Euroflax Sport Weight Linen Yarn*

SEWN AND STUFFED TOYS: *Liberty of London Tana Lawn Classics Cotton Fabric, Robert Kaufman Oxford Fabric, Moda French General Woven Dots and Stripes Fabric, Mary Flanagan Mini Textured Felted Wool Bundle, Manos Del Uruguay Maxima Yarn*

WOVEN CAMERA STRAP: *Louet Euroflax Sport Weight Linen Yarn*

ACKNOWLEDGMENTS

My gratitude goes to:

First, my friends who are the teachers in this book.

Anne McClain and Kate Miss, who also taught wonderful classes in my studio.

Everyone at the Textile Arts Center in Brooklyn, especially Owyn Ruck, for the perfect space in which to photograph.

Photographers Maria Alexandra Vettese and Stephanie Congdon Barnes, and their team, Arturo Cubria, Ryan Shimala, and Julia Ziegler-Haynes.

Joelle Hoverson, Jennifer Hoverson Jahnke, and Page Marchese Norman at Purl Soho for supplying beautiful materials.

June Okada, Rebekah Eshleman, Liza Steinberg Demby, Sarah Palmer, and Kamara Thomas for their help.

My editors, Liana Allday and Melanie Falick, and everyone at Stewart, Tabori & Chang.

Designer Brooke Hellewell Reynolds for bringing it all together.

And finally, Josh and Eli.

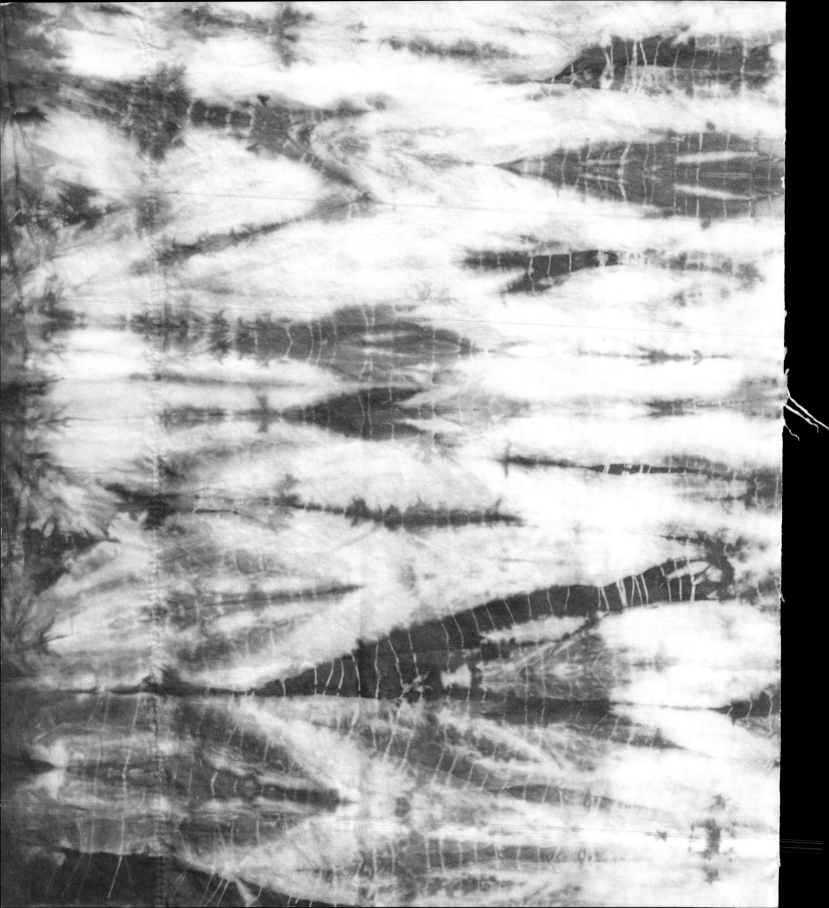